Wireshark Essentials

Get up and running with Wireshark to analyze network
packets and protocols effectively

James H. Baxter

[PACKT] open source✽
PUBLISHING   community experience distilled

BIRMINGHAM - MUMBAI

Wireshark Essentials

First published: October 2014

Production reference: 1211014

Published by Packt Publishing Ltd.
Livery Place
35 Livery Street
Birmingham B3 2PB, UK.

ISBN 978-1-78355-463-8

www.packtpub.com

Credits

Author
James H. Baxter

Reviewers
Sarath Lakshman
Bruno Vernay
Ms. Samia Yousif

Commissioning Editor
Pramila Balan

Acquisition Editor
Larissa Pinto

Content Development Editor
Sweny M. Sukumaran

Technical Editor
Shashank Desai

Copy Editor
Roshni Banerjee

Project Coordinator
Akash Poojary

Proofreaders
Simran Bhogal
Maria Gould
Ameesha Green
Paul Hindle

Indexers
Hemangini Bari
Rekha Nair

Graphics
Sheetal Aute
Abhinash Sahu

Production Coordinator
Nitesh Thakur

Cover Work
Nitesh Thakur

About the Author

James H. Baxter is the President and CEO of PacketIQ Inc., a company which specializes in network and application performance analysis and management, including development of advanced analysis frameworks and tools.

With over 30 years of experience in the IT industry, his diverse technical background includes electronics, RF, satellite, data/telecom, LAN/WAN and voice design, network management, speech technologies, and Java/.NET programming. For most of the last 20 years, he has been working specifically with network and application performance issues.

James is a Wireshark Certified Network Analyst (WCNA). He is a member of the IEEE, Computer Measurement Group, and Association of Computing Machinery, and he follows advancements in artificial intelligence.

James is also a private pilot who holds an amateur radio Extra class license. He is also a guitar player and an amateur astronomer. You can find out more about James and PacketIQ Inc. at www.packetiq.com.

About the Reviewers

Sarath Lakshman is a software engineer at Couchbase. He is a core developer for Couchbase MapReduce View Engine, and he works on storage and indexing problems at Couchbase. Before Couchbase, he worked at Zynga for over 2 years, building ZBase—a distributed storage platform that powered the entire social games infrastructure at Zynga. He was attracted to Linux in his teenage years, and he created a user-friendly Linux distribution called Slynux. He is also the author of *Linux Shell Scripting Cookbook*, *Packt Publishing*. He holds a Bachelor's degree in Computer Science from Model Engineering College, India. He is an open source software enthusiast and has contributed to various projects in the past. To find out more about Sarath, you can visit www.sarathlakshman.com.

Bruno Vernay has been working with all forms of web application design and development for the last 15 years—a bit of CSS/JavaScript and a lot of Java, SQL, Linux, and network. He even had the chance to work with Complex Event Processing, Rules Engines, and Geographic Information Systems. He also touched on large clusters as well as embedded devices and has been through various paradigms, from modeling via UML to Test or Domain Driven Development and Domain Specific Language. If he has time, he would like to work on Synthetic Biology and Biohacking. Now, he is focusing on IoT Security, enjoying the variety of systems and opportunities.

Ms. Samia Yousif holds Master's and Bachelor's degrees from the University of Bahrain as well as CCNA, CCNP, and CCDA from Bahrain Training Institute and Diploma Mr. Tabatabai in culture Quranic from Islamic Enlightenment Society. She has developed extensive knowledge and skills in various technical fields of Computer Science and IT. She has published conference publications and books and received the Research Award from Ahlia University and the e-Government Excellence Award (e-Education Award). She has delivered several IT workshops and has attended many seminars. Samia has 10 years of teaching experience at an undergraduate level in Computer Science and IT. Furthermore, she has worked on the development of numerous systems and professional website applications using the most up-to-date web technologies. She is now an Assistant Director of ICT at Ahlia University, Kingdom of Bahrain, and she is planning to undertake a PhD program.

She has contributed to the book *Computer Jobs & Certifications Choose & Improve Your IT Career, Dr. Mansoor Al-Aali, Lulu.com* and also reviewed the book *Packet Tracer Network Simulator, Jesin A, Packt Publishing*. She has also written a lab manual, *HTML Fundamental*, for the Royal University for Women in October 2006 and AMA International University, Bahrain, in May 2006.

To find out more about her, visit her website http://samiayousif.hostoi.com.

www.PacktPub.com

Support files, eBooks, discount offers, and more

For support files and downloads related to your book, please visit www.PacktPub.com.

Did you know that Packt offers eBook versions of every book published, with PDF and ePub files available? You can upgrade to the eBook version at www.PacktPub.com and as a print book customer, you are entitled to a discount on the eBook copy. Get in touch with us at service@packtpub.com for more details.

At www.PacktPub.com, you can also read a collection of free technical articles, sign up for a range of free newsletters and receive exclusive discounts and offers on Packt books and eBooks.

http://PacktLib.PacktPub.com

Do you need instant solutions to your IT questions? PacktLib is Packt's online digital book library. Here, you can search, access, and read Packt's entire library of books.

Why subscribe?

- Fully searchable across every book published by Packt
- Copy and paste, print, and bookmark content
- On demand and accessible via a web browser

Free access for Packt account holders

If you have an account with Packt at www.PacktPub.com, you can use this to access PacktLib today and view 9 entirely free books. Simply use your login credentials for immediate access.

Table of Contents

Preface

Wireshark is perhaps the world's most popular network packet analyzer used to troubleshoot and analyze network and application protocols across wide variety of technologies. Wireshark is free, open source, and available for Windows, Mac OS X, Linux, and several Unix-like platforms, and it is continuously being improved and expanded by its original developer, Gerald Combs, and over 500 code contributors.

Wireshark has a rich feature set, including the ability to capture, save, and import packet files in a variety of formats. It provides an extensive filtering capability, detailed protocol information, statistics, and built-in analysis and packet coloring features to help you identify and analyze important events. This powerful analysis capability is available to anyone who is willing to invest a little time to learn Wireshark's basic features and how to interpret a relatively small set of core network and application protocols.

This book is designed to introduce Wireshark and essential packet analysis techniques to not only network engineers and administrators, but also application developers, database designers and administrators, server administrators, and IT security professionals. It also gives them the essential knowledge and practical examples needed to effectively utilize Wireshark so they can include packet-level analysis in their daily tasks.

Application developers can use Wireshark to view and understand how the routines in their code that make network calls translate into request/response packets, inspect how the application-related data fields within those packets are structured, and verify that these calls are efficient and work in the way that they are anticipated and intended.

Database designers and administrators can utilize the packet details provided by Wireshark to examine the queries and responses carried by packets and to check whether they are efficient. Are there a lot of small request/response cycles involved in a transactional query that could be replaced by fewer, more efficient requests to improve performance?

Server processing times can be a huge factor and point of contention in performance-related issues across almost all IT arenas. This book will show you how easy it is to use Wireshark to identify and measure server processing times at the packet level where there can be no disputing the evidence.

IT security professionals inherently utilize protocol-level parameters to configure firewalls and intrusion detection and prevention devices, but may lack the skills to confidently establish and verify these factors themselves—instead relying upon others for this critical input. The ability of a security professional to inspect packet captures to identify, characterize, and guard against malicious traffic is assumed, and a small investment of time with this book will open the door to mastering this essential skill.

Finally, network support personnel are called upon on an almost daily basis to troubleshoot strange connectivity or slow network issues. They need the visibility and evidence that packet-level analysis provides to not only defend their domain, but also to assist in identifying and resolving the real problem; that's usually the only way the heat gets permanently turned off. Good Wireshark skills are a must-have for these folks.

The focus of this book is to teach you how to become comfortable and proficient in using basic Wireshark skills within your respective domain. At first glance, looking at a screen full of packets of seemingly endless varieties and sources can be very intimidating, but it is actually quite easy after learning the concepts provided in this book to isolate just the packets that pertain to the area of interest and filter everything else out, establish a high-level understanding of the packet flow and sequence of events, and then find and inspect the correct packets and data fields that address the issue at hand.

One of the additional advantages of learning how to use Wireshark is an increased understanding of how networks and applications really work, the benefits of which are helpful across all other aspects of your work. I'm confident the small investment in time required to learn Wireshark and packet analysis skills will return huge dividends.

What this book covers

Chapter 1, *Getting Acquainted with Wireshark*, starts with the first step. This introductory chapter will help you quickly start developing proficiency with Wireshark by getting it installed and doing something fun and useful, such as performing a packet capture, isolating and filtering some traffic of interest, and saving a trace file before diving into more details and the supporting concepts in the later chapters.

Chapter 2, *Networking for Packet Analysts*, provides an overview of network technologies, foundational network protocols including IP, UDP, and TCP, and how the most common protocols fit together within the OSI and DARPA model levels. The goal of this chapter is to develop a good mental model of how networks and protocols function together to allow you to confidently and effectively approach packet-level analysis.

Chapter 3, *Capturing All the Right Packets*, covers the details of how to correctly position Wireshark in the network and configure it to capture the desired packets, how to identify network conversations of interest and apply display filters to isolate just those packets, and finally save a filtered file for further or later analysis. These are the essential skills that support practical packet analysis.

Chapter 4, *Configuring Wireshark*, provides a number of features that can be configured and employed to enhance the accuracy and ease of analysis activities. The various ways to display and interpret packet timestamps are especially important and we'll cover these topics thoroughly, along with other essential configuration options, packet list coloring to help identify important events, and how to save different configurations in customized profiles that can be tailored and selected for various analysis tasks.

Chapter 5, *Network Protocols*, covers a number of other essential and useful network protocols that you should be familiar with, including ICMP, DNS, DHCP, an introductory review of Internet Protocol Version 6 (IPv6), and an example application layer protocol (HTTP). We will also discuss basic Wireshark capture and display filters.

Chapter 6, *Troubleshooting and Performance Analysis*, provides methodologies to apply your new skills and protocol knowledge to the primary purpose for which Wireshark was developed: troubleshooting and analyzing network and application issues and performance. We'll cover the top reasons for poor performance and how to use Wireshark to detect and measure them.

Chapter 7, Packet Analysis for Security Tasks, introduces the use of Wireshark to detect and analyze suspect traffic such as scans and sweeps, operating system fingerprinting, malformed packets, phone home traffic, and other unusual packets and patterns that could indicate malicious origin.

Chapter 8, Command-line and Other Utilities, covers some of the most useful command-line utilities provided with Wireshark to perform packet captures with minimal resources and to manipulate packet trace files. We will also discuss a few other tools that can help you round out your packet analysis toolset.

What you need for this book

To accomplish the tasks and repeat the examples provided in this book, you only need a computer on which you can install and use Wireshark and a wired LAN connection to your home or business network.

Although you could capture from a Wireless interface, the additional overhead of wireless management frames can be burdensome and distracting to analyze, so it's much better for your learning experience to start off on a wired network.

In terms of background knowledge, if you are involved in some aspect of the IT industry, you probably have at least some basic familiarity with the common concepts and terms used with packet-level analysis, such as switches, routers, packets, protocols, TCP/IP, and HTTP, but it is assumed that you possess only a basic familiarity with network and application protocols.

Who this book is for

This book is aimed at a broad spectrum of IT professionals who want to develop or enhance their Wireshark skills to expand their troubleshooting and analysis capabilities and increase their value in the workplace: network designers and administrators, application developers and support personnel, database designers and administrators, IT security professionals, and anyone else whose job responsibilities include supporting information technology in today's increasingly networked world.

Conventions

In this book, you will find a number of styles of text that distinguish between different kinds of information. Here are some examples of these styles, and an explanation of their meaning.

Code words in text, database table names, folder names, filenames, file extensions, pathnames, dummy URLs, user input, and Twitter handles are shown as follows: "The IP address of the target host was `10.1.1.125`."

A block of code is set as follows:

```
(tcp.flags&02 && tcp.seq==0) || (tcp.flags&12 && tcp.seq==0) || (tcp.
flags.ack && tcp.seq==1 && !tcp.nxtseq > 0 && !tcp.ack >1) || tcp.
flags.fin == 1 || tcp.flags.reset ==1
```

Any command-line input or output is written as follows:

```
dumpcap -i 2 -f "host 192.168.1.115" -w capture.pcapng
```

New terms and **important words** are shown in bold. Words that you see on the screen, in menus or dialog boxes for example, appear in the text like this: "This field is roughly equivalent to the **Time To Live** field in IPv4; it is decremented by one by each device that forwards the IPv6 packet."

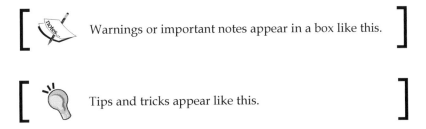

Warnings or important notes appear in a box like this.

Tips and tricks appear like this.

Reader feedback

Feedback from our readers is always welcome. Let us know what you think about this book—what you liked or may have disliked. Reader feedback is important for us to develop titles that you really get the most out of.

To send us general feedback, simply send an e-mail to `feedback@packtpub.com`, and mention the book title via the subject of your message.

If there is a topic that you have expertise in and you are interested in either writing or contributing to a book, see our author guide on `www.packtpub.com/authors`.

Customer support

Now that you are the proud owner of a Packt book, we have a number of things to help you to get the most from your purchase.

Errata

Although we have taken every care to ensure the accuracy of our content, mistakes do happen. If you find a mistake in one of our books—maybe a mistake in the text or the code—we would be grateful if you would report this to us. By doing so, you can save other readers from frustration and help us improve subsequent versions of this book. If you find any errata, please report them by visiting http://www.packtpub. com/submit-errata, selecting your book, clicking on the **errata submission form** link, and entering the details of your errata. Once your errata are verified, your submission will be accepted and the errata will be uploaded on our website, or added to any list of existing errata, under the Errata section of that title. Any existing errata can be viewed by selecting your title from http://www.packtpub.com/support.

Piracy

Piracy of copyright material on the Internet is an ongoing problem across all media. At Packt, we take the protection of our copyright and licenses very seriously. If you come across any illegal copies of our works, in any form, on the Internet, please provide us with the location address or website name immediately so that we can pursue a remedy.

Please contact us at copyright@packtpub.com with a link to the suspected pirated material.

We appreciate your help in protecting our authors, and our ability to bring you valuable content.

Questions

You can contact us at questions@packtpub.com if you are having a problem with any aspect of the book, and we will do our best to address it.

1
Getting Acquainted with Wireshark

Since its creation in 1997 by Gerald Combs to troubleshoot network problems at a small ISP, Wireshark (originally called Ethereal) has now become one of the most popular tools available for packet-level analysis of network and application protocols. This is mostly because it is an open source solution, which makes it freely available to any technical professional, as well as its extensive range of features, coverage of over 1000 protocols, and the continued support and improvements made possible by contributions from over 800 developers around the globe.

This introductory chapter will help you to quickly become proficient in Wireshark by installing it on your system and doing something fun and useful with it, before diving into more details and supporting concepts.

In this chapter, we will cover the following topics:

- Installing Wireshark
- Performing a packet capture
- Wireshark user interface essentials
- Using display filters to isolate traffic of interest
- Saving a filtered packet trace file

The chapters that follow will build on and provide the supporting concepts for these basic functions to allow you to develop the Wireshark skills that are most applicable to your technical role and objectives.

Installing Wireshark

Wireshark can be installed on machines running 32- and 64-bit Windows (XP, Win7, Win8.1, and so on), Mac OS X (10.5 and higher), and most flavors of Linux/Unix. Installation on Windows and Mac machines is quick and easy because installers are available from the Wireshark website download page. Wireshark is a standard package available on many Linux distributions, and there is a list of links to third-party installers provided on the Wireshark download page for a variety of popular *nix platforms. Alternatively, you can download the source code and compile Wireshark for your environment if a precompiled installation package isn't available.

Wireshark relies on the WinPcap (Windows) or libpcap (Linux/Unix/Mac) libraries to provide the packet capture and capture filtering functions; the appropriate library is installed during the Wireshark installation.

 You might need administrator (Windows) or root (Linux/Unix/Mac) privileges to install Wireshark and the WinPcap/libpcap utilities on your workstation.

Assuming that you're installing Wireshark on a Windows or Mac machine, you need to go to the Wireshark website (`https://www.wireshark.org/`) and click on the **Download** button at the top of the page. This will take you to the download page, and at the same time attempt to perform an autodiscovery of your operating system type and version from your browser info. The majority of the time, the correct Wireshark installation package for your machine will be highlighted, and you only have to click on the highlighted link to download the correct installer.

 If you already have Wireshark installed, an autoupdate feature will notify you of available version updates when you launch Wireshark.

Installing Wireshark on Windows

In the following screenshot, the Wireshark download page has identified that a 64-bit Windows installer is appropriate for this Windows workstation:

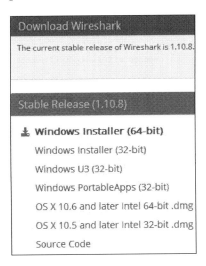

Clicking on the highlighted link downloads a `Wireshark-win64-1.10.8.exe` file or similar executable file that you can save on your hard drive. Double-clicking on the executable starts the installation process. You need to follow these steps:

1. Agree to the **License Agreement**.

2. Accept all of the defaults by clicking on **Next** for each prompt, including the prompt to install WinPcap, which is a library needed to capture packets from the **Network Interface Card** (**NIC**) on your workstation.

3. Early in the Wireshark installation, the process will pause and prompt you to click on **Install** and several **Next** buttons in separate windows to install WinPcap.

4. After the WinPcap installation is complete, click through the remaining **Next** prompts to finish the Wireshark installation.

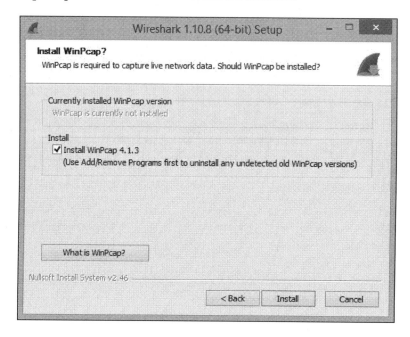

Installing Wireshark on Mac OS X

The process to install Wireshark on Mac is the same as the process for Windows, except that you will not be prompted to install WinPcap; libpcap, the packet capture library for Mac and *nix machines, gets installed instead (without prompting).

There are, however, two additional requirements that may need to be addressed in a Mac installation:

- The first is to install X11, a windowing system library. If this is needed for your system, you will be informed and provided a link that ultimately takes you to the XQuartz project download page so you can install this package.

- The second requirement that might come up is if upon starting Wireshark, you are informed that there are no interfaces on which a capture can be done. This is a permissions issue on the **Berkeley packet filter** (BPF) that can be resolved by opening a terminal window and typing the following command:

```
bash-3.2$ sudo chmod 644 /dev/bpf*
```

If this process needs to be repeated each time you start Wireshark, you can perform a web search for a more permanent permissions solution for your environment.

Installing Wireshark on Linux/Unix

The requirements and process to install Wireshark on a Linux or Unix platform can vary significantly depending on the particular environment. Wireshark is usually available by default through the package management systems for your specific Linux distribution. Guidance to install Wireshark on Linux can be found in *Chapter 2*, *Networking for Packet Analysts*, or in the Wireshark user documentation located at www.wireshark.org/docs/wsug_html_chunked/ChapterBuildInstall.html.

Performing your first packet capture

When you first start Wireshark, you are presented with an initial **Start Page** as shown in the following screenshot:

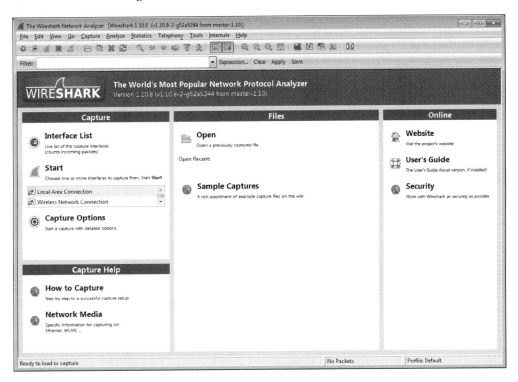

Don't get too fond of this screen. Although you'll see this every time you start Wireshark, once you do a capture, open a trace file, or perform any other function within Wireshark, this screen will be replaced with the standard Wireshark user interface and you won't see it again until the next time you start Wireshark. So, we won't spend much time here.

Selecting a network interface

If you have a number of network interfaces on your machine, you may not be sure which one to select to capture packets, but there's a fairly easy way to figure this out. On the Wireshark start page, click on **Interface List** (alternatively, click on **Interfaces** from the **Capture** menu or click on the first icon on the icon bar).

The **Wireshark Capture Interfaces** window that opens provides a list and description of all the network interfaces on your machine, the IP address assigned to each one (if an address has been assigned), and a couple of counters, such as the total number of packets seen on the interface since this window opened and a packets/s (packets per second) counter. If an interface has an IPv6 address assigned (which may start with `fe80::` and contain a number of colons) and this is being displayed, you can click on the IPv6 address and it will toggle to display the IPv4 address. This is shown in the following screenshot:

 On Linux/Unix/Mac platforms, you might also see a loopback interface that can be selected to capture packets being sent between applications on the same machine. However, in most cases, you'll only be interested in capturing packets from a network interface.

The goal is to identify the active interface that will be used to communicate with the Internet when you open a browser and navigate to a website. If you have a wired local area network connection and the interface is enabled, that's probably the active interface, but you might also have a wireless interface that is enabled and you may or may not be the primary interface. The most reliable indicator of the active network interface is that it will have greater number of steadily increasing packets with a corresponding active number of packets/s (which will vary over time). Another possible indicator is if an interface has an IP address assigned and others do not. If you're still unsure, open a browser window and navigate to one of your favorite websites and watch the packets and packets/s counters to identify the interface that shows the greatest increase in activity.

Performing a packet capture

Once you've identified the correct interface, select the checkbox on the left-hand side of that interface and click on the **Start** button at the bottom of the **Capture Interfaces** window. Wireshark will start capturing all the packets that can be seen from that interface, including the packets sent to and from your workstation. You'll see a bewildering variety of packets going by in the top section (called the **Packet List** pane) of the screen; this is normal. If you don't see this, try a different interface.

It's a bit amazing just how much background traffic there is on a typical network, such as broadcast packets from devices advertising their names, addresses, and services to and from other devices asking for addresses of stations they want to communicate with. Also, a fair amount of traffic is generated from your own workstation for applications and services that are running in the background, and you had no idea they were creating this much noise. Your Wireshark's **Packet List** pane may look similar to the following screenshot; however, we can ignore all this for now:

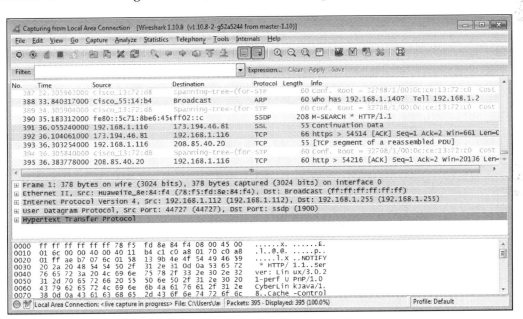

We're ready to generate some traffic that we'll be interested in analyzing. Open a new Internet browser window, enter www.wireshark.org in the address box, and press *Enter*.

When the https://www.wireshark.org/ home page finishes loading, stop the Wireshark capture by either selecting **Stop** from the **Capture** menu or by clicking on the red square stop icon that's between the **View** and **Go** menu headers.

Wireshark user interface essentials

Once you have completed your first capture, you will see the normal Wireshark user interface main screen. So before we go much further, a quick introduction to the primary parts of this user interface will be helpful so you'll know what's being referred to as we continue the analysis process.

There are eight significant sections or elements of the default Wireshark user interface, as shown in the following screenshot:

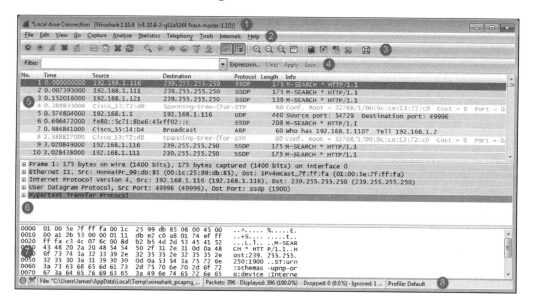

Let's look at the eight significant sections in detail:

- **Title**: This area reflects the interface from where a capture is being taken or the filename of an open packet trace file

- **Menu**: This is the standard row of main functions and subfunctions in Wireshark

- **Main toolbar (icons)**: These provide a quick way to access the most useful Wireshark functions and are well worth getting familiar with and using

- **Display filter toolbar**: This allows you to quickly create, edit, clear, apply, and save filters to isolate packets of interest for analysis

- **Packet list pane**: This section contains a summary info line for each captured packet, as well as a packet number and relative timestamp

- **Packet details pane**: This section provides a hierarchical display of information about a single packet that has been selected in the packet list pane, which is divided into sections for the various protocols contained in a packet

- **Packet bytes pane**: This section displays the selected packets' contents in hex bytes or bits form, as well as an ASCII display of the data that can be helpful

- **Status bar**: This section provides an expert info indicator, edit capture comments icon, trace file path name and size information, data on the number of packets captured and displayed and other info, and a profile display and selection section

Filtering out the noise

Somewhere in your packet capture, there are packets involved with loading the Wireshark home page—but how do you find and view just those packets out of all the background noise?

The simplest and most reliable method is to determine the IP address of the Wireshark website and filter out all the packets except those flowing between that IP address and the IP address of your workstation by using a display filter. The best approach—and the one that you'll likely use as a first step for most of your post-capture analysis work in future—is to investigate a list of all the conversations by IP address and/or hostnames, sorted by the most active nodes, and identify your target hostname, website name, or IP address from this list.

From the Wireshark menu, select **Conversations** from the **Statistics** menu, and in the **Conversations** window that opens, select the **IPv4** tab at the top. You'll see a list of network conversations identified by **Address A** and **Address B**, with columns for total **Packets**, **Bytes**, **Packets A→B**, **Bytes A→B**, **Packets A←B**, and **Bytes A←B**.

Scrolling over to the right-hand side of this window, there are **Relative Start** values. These are the times when each particular conversation was first observed in the capture, relative to the start of the capture in seconds. The next column is **Duration**, which is how long this conversation persisted in the capture (first to last packet seen).

Finally, there are average data rates in **bits per second (bps)** in each direction for each conversation, which is the network impact for this conversation. All these are shown in the following screenshot:

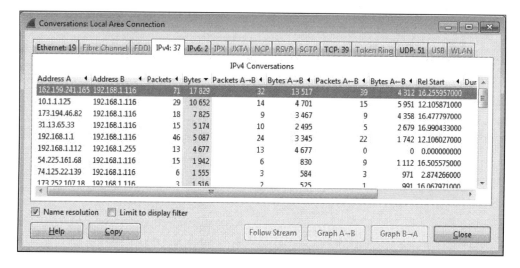

We want to sort the list of conversations to get the busiest ones—called the Top Talkers in network jargon—at the top of the list. Click on the **Bytes** column header and then click on it again. Your list should look something like the preceding screenshot, and if you didn't get a great deal of other background traffic flowing to/from your workstation, the traffic from `https://www.wireshark.org/` should have the greatest volume and therefore be at the top of the list.

In this example, the conversation between IP addresses **162.159.241.165** and **192.168.1.116** has the greatest overall volume, and looking at the **Bytes A->B** column, it's apparent that the majority of the traffic was from the **162.159.241.165** address to the **192.168.1.116** address. However, at this point, how do we know if this is really the conversation that we're after?

We will need to resolve the IP addresses from our list to hostnames or website addresses, and this can be done from within Wireshark by turning on **Network Name Resolution** and trying to get hostnames and/or website addresses resolved for those IP addresses using reverse DNS queries (using what is known as a pointer (PTR) DNS record type). If you just installed or started Wireshark, the **Name Resolution** option may not be turned on by default.

This is usually a good thing, as Wireshark can create traffic of its own by transmitting the DNS queries trying to resolve all the IP addresses that it comes across during the capture, and you don't really want that going on during a capture. However, the **Name Resolution** option can be very helpful to resolve IP addresses to proper hostnames after a capture is complete.

To enable **Name Resolution**, navigate to **View | Name Resolution | Enable for Network Layer** (click to turn on the checkmark) and make sure **Use External Network Name Resolver** is enabled as well. Wireshark will attempt to resolve all the IP addresses in the capture to their hostname or website address, and the resolved names will then appear (replacing the previous IP addresses) in the packet list as well as the **Conversations** window.

Note that the **Name Resolution** option at the bottom of the **Conversations** window must be enabled as well (it usually is by default), and this setting affects whether resolved names or IP addresses appear in the **Conversations** window (if **Name Resolution** is enabled in the Wireshark main screen), as shown in the following screenshot:

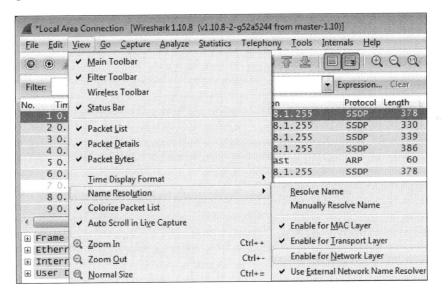

At this point, you should see the conversation pair between **wireshark.org** and your workstation at or near the top of the list, as shown in the following screenshot. Of course, your workstation will have a different name or may only appear as an IP address, but identifying the conversation to **wireshark.org** has been achieved.

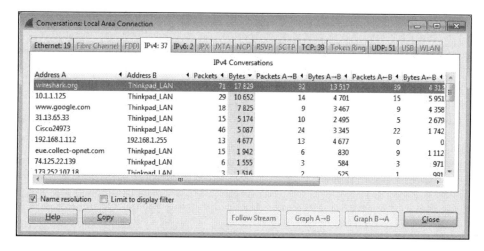

Applying a display filter

You now want to see just the conversation between your workstation and **wireshark. org**, and get rid of all the extraneous conversations so you can focus on the traffic of interest. This is accomplished by creating a filter that only displays the desired traffic.

Right-click on the line containing the **wireshark.org** entry and navigate to **Apply as Filter | Selected | A<->B**, as shown in the following screenshot:

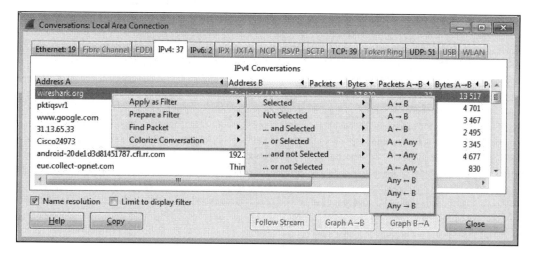

Wireshark will create and apply a display filter string that isolates the displayed traffic to just the conversation between the IP addresses of **wireshark.org** and your workstation, as shown in the following screenshot. Note that if you create or edit a display filter entry manually, you will need to click on **Apply** to apply the filter to the trace file (or **Clear** to clear it).

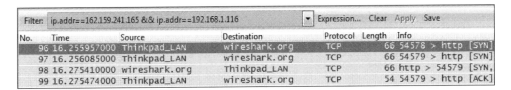

This particular display filter syntax works with IP addresses, not with hostnames, and uses an `ip.addr==` (IP address equals) syntax for each node along with the `&&` (and) logic operator to build a string that says `display any packet that contains this IP address *and* that IP address`. This is the type of display filter that you will be using a great deal for packet analysis.

You'll notice as you scroll up and down in the **Packet List** pane that all the other packets, except those between your workstation and **wireshark.org**, are gone. They're not gone in the strict sense, they're just hidden—as you can observe by inspecting the **Packet No.** column, there are gaps in the numbering sequence; those are for the hidden packets.

Saving the packet trace

Now that you've isolated the traffic of interest using a display filter, you can save a new packet trace file that contains just the filtered packets.

This serves two purposes. Firstly, you can close Wireshark, come back to it later, open the filtered trace file, and pick up where you left off in your analysis, as well as have a record of the capture in case you need to reference it later such as in a troubleshooting scenario.

Secondly, it's much easier and quicker to work in the various Wireshark screens and functions with a smaller, more focused trace file that contains just the packets that you want to analyze.

To create a new packet trace file containing just the filtered/displayed packets, select **Export Specified Packets** from the Wireshark **File** menu.

You can navigate to and/or create a folder to hold your Wireshark trace files, and then enter a filename for the trace file that you want to save. In this example, the filename is `wireshark_website.pcapng`. By default, Wireshark will save the trace file in the pcapng format (which is the preferred format). If you don't specify a file extension with the filename, Wireshark will provide the appropriate extension based on the **Save as type** selection, as shown in the following screenshot:

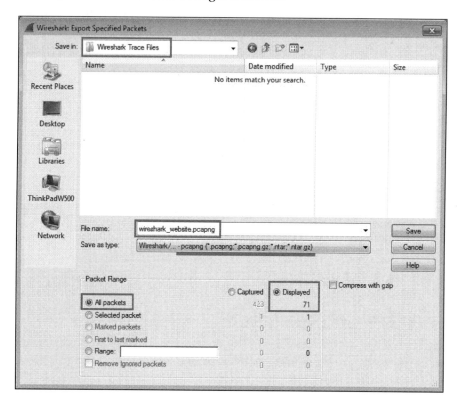

Also, by default, Wireshark will have the **All packets** option selected, and if a display filter is applied (as it is in this scenario), the **Displayed** option will be selected as opposed to the **Captured** option that saves all the packets regardless of whether a filter was applied. Having entered a filename and confirmed that all the save selections are correct, you can click on **Save** to save the new packet trace file.

Note that when you have finished this trace file save activity, Wireshark still has all the original packets from the capture in memory, and they can still be viewed by clicking on **Clear** in the **Display Filter Toolbar** menu. If you want to work further with the new trace file you just saved, you'll need to open it by clicking on **Open** in the **File** menu (or **Open Recent** in the **File** menu).

Summary

Congratulations! If you accomplished all the activities covered in this chapter, you have successfully installed Wireshark, performed a packet capture, created a filter to isolate and display just the packets you were interested in from all the extraneous noise, and created a new packet trace file containing just those packets so you can analyze them later. Moreover, in the process, you gained an initial familiarity with the Wireshark user interface and you learned how to use several of its most useful and powerful features. Not bad for a first chapter.

In the next chapter, we'll review some essential network concepts needed to provide a solid foundation to perform packet-level analysis. The main goal of the next chapter is to help you develop a mental model of networking that lends itself well to packet-level analysis without getting too tangled up in unnecessary details.

2
Networking for Packet Analysts

Packet analysis is all about analyzing how applications transfer useful data from point A to point B over networks. So, an understanding of how networks function is essential.

In this chapter, we will cover the following topics:

- Why the seven-layer OSI model matters
- IP networks and subnets
- Switching and routing packets
- Ethernet frames and switches
- IP addresses and routers
- WAN links
- Wireless networking

The seven-layer OSI model will be mapped to the most common networking terms, and we'll review frames, switching, IP addressing, routing, and a few other networking topics of interest. The goal is to develop a mental model of networking that lends itself well to packet-level analysis.

The OSI model – why it matters

The **Open Systems Interconnections (OSI)** reference model is an industry recognized standard developed by the **International Organization for Standardization (ISO)** to divide networking functions into seven logical layers to support and encourage (relatively) independent development while providing (relatively) seamless interconnectivity between each layer from different hardware/software environments, platforms, and vendors. There's also a somewhat simpler four-layer **Defense Advanced Research Projects Agency (DARPA)** model that maps to the OSI model, but the OSI version is the most commonly referred to. I'll reference both models when discussing the various layers.

The following diagram compares the OSI and DARPA reference models:

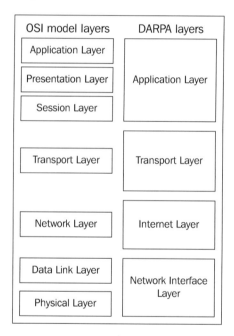

Unless you're in the business of writing protocols, there's no need to study any of the seven layers in great depth, but it is helpful to understand them conceptually because these layers are referred to by the industry and your IT peers.

More importantly, it's essential that you know where and how these layers and their associated protocols are presented in Wireshark's **Packet Details** pane. We'll cover the layers from this aspect to help you remember them and get the most use from the discussion.

Understanding network protocols

Network protocols, like the OSI layers, are a set of industry standard rules and designs used to exchange messages and data between computers and applications. In any discussion about OSI layers, you are directly or indirectly referring to the protocols associated with a given layer—the most commonly known protocols are IP, UDP, TCP, HTTP, and so on—and the significant functions they perform.

For example, you'll often hear the terms network layer and IP layer used interchangeably, and it is assumed and understood that you are talking about the layer and the associated protocol that contains and uses IP addresses to route packets from point A to point B across the network. The discussions that follow will tie the OSI and DARPA layers to their associated protocols.

The seven OSI layers

As we cover the OSI layers starting from layer 1 and working up to layer 7, I'll outline how each layer's associated protocol(s) are displayed in Wireshark and/or used in networking hardware. The mental model you develop from this approach should be the most accurate and useful for packet analysis.

Layer 1 – the physical layer

The physical layer encompasses the electrical characteristics and mechanical standards to get data bits transmitted from a computer's **Network Interface Card (NIC)** to a switch port or between switch and router ports. The most common standards, terms, and devices you'll encounter at this layer include the following:

- **Ethernet**: This is a family of networking technologies for **local area networks (LANs)**.
- **RJ-45**: These are 8-pin modular connectors found on both ends of a copper Ethernet cable that are plugged into the NIC on a computer and a wall jack or switch port
- **Cat 5 (Cat 5e or Cat 6) cables**: These are Ethernet cables that use twisted-pair copper wires. "Cat" stands for the category of cable and reflects its quality and data speed capabilities.
- **100Base-T, 1000Base-T, and 1000Base-LX**: These represent a particular Ethernet standard. 100Base-T is 100 Mbps over twisted-pair cable using RJ-45 connectors, 1000Base-LX is 1000 Mbps over fiber, and so on.
- **Single-mode and multimode fiber optic cables**: These use pulses of light from solid-state LEDs or lasers to transmit data bits.

The Ethernet standards used to connect NICs to switches are also used to connect switches together and to connect switches to routers or other network devices, although the cables and connectors used may vary depending on cable type and speed.

There are other layer 1 standards in common use, including 802.11 Wireless, Frame Relay, and ATM; the last two are used in long distance **wide area networks (WANs)**.

Layer 2 – the data-link layer

The data-link layer organizes raw bits from the physical layer (typically Ethernet) into frames, which is the first manifestation of what is generally called a packet that you'll see in Wireshark. This layer is a dividing line between physical networking, electrical/mechanical standards, and the logical structures (protocols) used to format and transmit, receive, and decode packets of data in the higher layers.

In the DARPA reference model, the physical and data-link OSI layers are combined and called the network interface layer. The significant features and functions of this layer (for Ethernet II frames) include:

- **Media Access Control (MAC) addresses**: These are the network addresses used in LANs. They are 6-byte network hardware addresses burned into memory chips on NICs, switches, routers, or other network device ports/interfaces:
    - The first three bytes of a MAC address are assigned to and can be associated with a specific manufacturer. Wireshark has a list of these and can display MAC addresses as a combination of the manufacturer code and the last three bytes. The manufacturer creates a unique last-three-bytes address for every interface so that each MAC address is unique across the globe. (Although, an NIC might be programmed to use another arbitrary MAC address, which is done for MAC spoofing for malicious attacks. But this is a very bad idea as another card may be using the same address and can cause a loss of data and some very confusing packet switching problems.)
    - Ethernet frames include a destination and source MAC address. MAC addresses are used to switch (not route – we'll make the distinction shortly) frames between computers on the same LAN or between computers and a router or other device port on a LAN.

- **Type (or EtherType) field**: This indicates the next higher protocol layer (typically IP (0800) or ARP (0806)). Wireshark uses this to determine the next protocol dissector to apply in packet decodes.
- **Payload**: This is the packet or datagram carried by the Ethernet frame.

- **The frame check sequence**: This is a 4-byte **Cyclic Redundancy Check (CRC)** error-detection code calculated from all the bits in a frame and added to the end of the frame. This is used to detect frames that have been corrupted usually because of faulty cables, noise induced on the wires in a cable from outside electrical signals, and so on. When a frame is received, this code is recalculated based on the bits received and compared to the FCS field. The bad frames are then discarded.

The following diagram illustrates the layout of the fields in an Ethernet frame:

c8 d7 19 21 b7 ec	00 1c 25 99 db 85	08 00	IP, ARP, etc.	46 55 e8 de
Destination MAC Addr	Source MAC Addr	EtherType	Payload	CRC Checksum
	MAC Header (14 bytes)		Datagram (46 - 1500 bytes)	FCS (4 bytes)

Ethernet Type II Frame
(64 - 1518 bytes)

A key point here — and this is important to understand — is that Ethernet frames and their MAC addresses are only able to transmit frames between devices on the local area network (LAN and IP subnet) they belong to.

Routers form the boundary between LANs by virtue of their IP subnet (subnetwork) addressing. All the devices belonging to the same IP subnet are part of the same LAN, and getting packets to or from a different subnet requires a router.

Once a frame enters a router port to get routed to a different/distant network, the Ethernet frame with its MAC addresses and FCS is stripped off and discarded. The payload inside the frame is routed to the port and it will leave on its way to the next device, and another frame with a different MAC address and recalculated FCS is created to encase the packet. This frame is then transmitted to the next destination.

The network devices that work at this layer — usually switches — are commonly referred to as layer 2 devices or layer 2 switches.

Finally, you should be aware that layer 2 switches can support several networking enhancements such as **Virtual LAN (VLAN)** and **Class of Service (CoS)** tagging, which is accomplished by adding a 4-byte 802.1Q field between the MAC addresses and EtherType field. You might see these frames between switches (but not on user ports).

VLAN is a layer 2 solution that allows administrative partitioning of various ports on a switch into separate broadcast domains. Devices located on different VLANs are effectively isolated from each other as if they were on separate physical networks. VLANs can be dispersed across multiple switches without running separate cables for each VLAN if the switches support VLAN tagging. Communication between devices on separate VLANs generally requires using a router.

In the following Wireshark packet details screenshot, the Ethernet II frame **Destination** and **Source** MAC addresses, **Type** (indicating that the next layer protocol is IP), and **Frame check sequence** are circled, as is the **Frame** summary.

 Wireshark displays a summary of each frame that includes frame sizes, captured timestamps and interframe times, and other useful information. This is metadata calculated by Wireshark to aid in analysis and not a part of the captured frame.

The following screenshot highlights the significant fields of an Ethernet frame:

 Any additional analysis provided by Wireshark in any area of the **Packet Details** pane that is calculated or otherwise not part of actual packet contents will be encased in brackets.

Layer 3 – the network layer

The network layer (called the Internet layer in the DARPA model) primarily handles the routing of packets across and to other networks along the path from source computers to destination hosts based on the destination IP address. The two most common protocols seen at this layer are Internet Protocol and Address Resolution Protocol.

Internet Protocol

The most common protocol in use at this layer is **Internet Protocol Version 4 (IPv4)**, which includes several essential fields to accomplish the task of routing packets across networks:

- **Differentiated Services (DiffServ)**: This field supports an enhancement to the IP that is generally called **Quality of Service (QoS)** and allows classification of certain types of traffic (voice, video, and so on) so that these packets can receive priority handling in cases of network congestion.

- **Total length**: This is the total length of the packet (minus the Ethernet MAC header).

- **Identification (IP ID)**: This an incrementing number used to support fragmentation.

- **Flags**: These are used to support fragmenting (dividing a packet into two or more smaller ones) in case the large packets have to be divided into several smaller ones to traverse a packet-size-limited link. These flags along with the IP ID field values allow proper reassembly of the fragmented packets into the original.

- **Fragment offset**: If the **Flag** field is **1** (more fragments), the value in this field indicates the offset from the start of the original payload in bytes that this fragment packet contains.

- **Time to Live (TTL)**: This is a "hop" or time counter that is decremented every time a packet passes through a router. If the TTL reaches zero, the packet is discarded. The primary purpose is to keep packets from living forever and crashing the network in the case of an inadvertent path loop.

- **Protocol**: This identifies the protocol in the IP packet's payload. Wireshark uses this to determine the next protocol dissector to apply to packet decodes.

- **Source and destination IP addresses**: These are the IP addresses of the sending machine and the ultimate destination machine. IP addresses are 4 bytes long and are represented as four octets (numbered 0 through 255 decimal) separated by periods.

In the following screenshot, the significant IPv4 fields are circled. These are the fields you'll want to inspect and be comfortable with when doing packet analysis at this layer.

```
⊞ Frame 7: 674 bytes on wire (5392 bits), 674 bytes captured (5392 bits) on interface 0
⊞ Ethernet II, Src: HonHaiPr_99:db:85 (00:1c:25:99:db:85), Dst: CiscoCon_21:b7:ec (c8:d7:19:21:b7:ec)
⊟ Internet Protocol Version 4, Src: 192.168.1.116 (192.168.1.116), Dst: 162.159.241.165 (162.159.241.165)
    Version: 4
    Header length: 20 bytes
  ⊟ Differentiated Services Field: 0x00 (DSCP 0x00: Default; ECN: 0x00: Not-ECT (Not ECN-Capable Transport))
      0000 00.. = Differentiated Services Codepoint: Default (0x00)
      .... ..00 = Explicit Congestion Notification: Not-ECT (Not ECN-Capable Transport) (0x00)
    Total Length: 660
    Identification: 0x30a0 (12448)
  ⊟ Flags: 0x02 (Don't Fragment)
      0... .... = Reserved bit: Not set
      .1.. .... = Don't fragment: Set
      ..0. .... = More fragments: Not set
    Fragment offset: 0
    Time to live: 128
    Protocol: TCP (6)
  ⊞ Header checksum: 0x0000 [validation disabled]
    Source: 192.168.1.116 (192.168.1.116)
    Destination: 162.159.241.165 (162.159.241.165)
⊞ Transmission Control Protocol, Src Port: 54579 (54579), Dst Port: http (80), Seq: 1, Ack: 1, Len: 616
⊞ Hypertext Transfer Protocol
```

Address Resolution Protocol

Another protocol you'll see at the network layer is **Address Resolution Protocol** (**ARP**), which is used by a device to obtain the MAC address of another device when it only knows that device's IP address.

In the following Wireshark packet details screenshot, note that the Ethernet frame destination MAC address is **Broadcast (ff:ff:ff:ff:ff:ff)**, **Type** is **ARP (0x0806)**, and the station has provided its own MAC and IP address in the ARP protocol **Sender** fields (which other stations listen to and use to build a table of MAC and IP addresses). It provides the IP address of the target device and puts all zeros in the **Target MAC Address** field. The target device should return a similar ARP packet addressed to the requestor with its MAC address in the **Sender** field.

A station will send an ARP request only in the following situations:

- The station that requires a MAC address for a target device hasn't heard a previous broadcast of that station's MAC address, or its ARP table has timed out (ARP entries are only kept for a period).

- The station that requires a MAC address for a target device has calculated (from the target's IP address and its own subnet mask) that the target device should be on the same LAN. Otherwise, the station assumes the target device is on a different network and sends its first session initiation packet to the default gateway (router) MAC address based on the entry in the sending station's default gateway configuration setting. The default gateway will forward the packet to the appropriate egress port to route it to the destination.

- The station that needs to send a packet to a distant network doesn't know the MAC address of its default gateway (for example, just after a power-up).

The following screenshot highlights the significant fields of an ARP packet:

```
⊞ Frame 35692: 60 bytes on wire (480 bits), 60 bytes captured (480 bits) on interface 0
⊟ Ethernet II, Src: Cisco_55:14:b4 (00:27:0d:55:14:b4), Dst: Broadcast (ff:ff:ff:ff:ff:ff)
  ⊞ Destination: Broadcast (ff:ff:ff:ff:ff:ff)
  ⊞ Source: Cisco_55:14:b4 (00:27:0d:55:14:b4)
    Type: ARP (0x0806)
    Padding: 000000000000000000000000000000000000
⊟ Address Resolution Protocol (request)
    Hardware type: Ethernet (1)
    Protocol type: IP (0x0800)
    Hardware size: 6
    Protocol size: 4
    Opcode: request (1)
    Sender MAC address: Cisco_55:14:b4 (00:27:0d:55:14:b4)
    Sender IP address: 192.168.1.2 (192.168.1.2)
    Target MAC address: 00:00:00_00:00:00 (00:00:00:00:00:00)
    Target IP address: 192.168.1.107 (192.168.1.107)
```

Other protocols utilized at this layer include **Internet Control Message Protocol (ICMP)**, which is used to send network error messages between devices, and **Internet Group Management Protocol (IGMP)**, which is used by hosts and adjacent routers to establish multicast (one-to-many) group memberships for network applications such as streaming video and gaming.

Layer 4 – the transport layer

The transport layer, as it's called in both the OSI and DARPA models, is responsible for transporting packets of data in unique sessions between applications or a user and an application by means of port numbers. The combination of a device or user's IP address and that device or user's assigned port number (referred to as a socket) will be different from another devices or users' IP address and port numbers (on the client side).

If the source host for a packet is a server, the source port is likely to be a well-known number for standard applications and services, such as port 80 for HTTP.

The transport layer typically uses one of two protocols, User Datagram Protocol or Transmission Control Protocol, with the latter being the more prevalent for most applications.

User Datagram Protocol

The **User Datagram Protocol** (**UDP**) is a fairly simple protocol. It is considered an *unreliable* transport as there's no guarantee of packet delivery or ordering, but it has lower overhead and is used by time-sensitive applications such as voice and video traffic, as well as by network services applications such as DNS.

The UDP header is only 8 bytes long and consists of the following:

- **Source and Destination port number**:These are 2 bytes each.

- **Length**: This is the length of the UDP header plus the payload. This is a 2-byte field.

- **Checksum**: This is the 2-byte field used to check errors of the UDP header and data. If no checksum was generated by the transmitter, this will be all zeros.

The following screenshot shows the fields contained in a UDP header:

```
⊞ Frame 18: 214 bytes on wire (1712 bits), 214 bytes captured (1712 bits)
⊞ Ethernet II, Src: Polycom_82:92:20 (00:04:f2:82:92:20), Dst: Cisco_55:14:b5 (00:27:0d:55:14:b5)
⊞ Internet Protocol Version 4, Src: 10.1.1.100 (10.1.1.100), Dst: 208.73.144.71 (208.73.144.71)
⊟ User Datagram Protocol, Src Port: 2222 (2222), Dst Port: 24268 (24268)
     Source port: 2222 (2222)
     Destination port: 24268 (24268)
     Length: 180
  ⊞ Checksum: 0xb64c
⊞ Real-Time Transport Protocol
```

Transmission Control Protocol

Unlike UDP, the **Transmission Control Protocol** (**TCP**) provides reliable delivery of data by detecting lost, duplicated, or out-of-order packets, requesting retransmission of lost data, or rearranging packets in the right order before delivering them to the application. TCP can also accept a large chunk of data from an application and handle getting the data transported to the other end reliably using multiple packets and reassembling them at the other end (as can UDP, but not reliably; the application has to determine and recover from lost packets).

The TCP header contents and length can vary depending on the options that may be in use, but in its simplest implementation, it consists of:

- **Source and Destination ports (2 bytes each)**: These are well-known registered ports that are used (on servers) to access standard application services such as HTTP, FTP, SMTP, databases, and so on. Port numbers assigned to client/user sessions are usually in a higher number range and assigned sequentially.

- **Sequence number (4 bytes)**: This is a number that represents the first octet in any given segment. Sequence numbers are initialized at the beginning of new sessions as a random number, and then incremented as data bytes and sent.

- **Acknowledgment number (4 bytes)**: When the ACK flag bit is set, this field contains the next sequence number expected from the sender, which in turn acknowledges receipt of all the bytes received up to that point.

The use of sequence and acknowledgment numbers are how the TCP ensures reliable delivery of data by tracking the number and order of received bytes.

Sequence and acknowledgment numbers are large and difficult for humans to follow; Wireshark can convert and display these as relative values that start with 0 at the beginning of a session to make it easier to inspect them and relate the values to the number of bytes transmitted and received.

- **Flags (9 bits)**: These bits are used to control connection setups, terminations, and flow control mechanisms.

- **Window size (2 bytes)**: This indicates the current size of the buffer on this host used to store received data until it can be handed off to the receiving application. This information lets the sending host adjust data flow rates in case of network or host congestion.

The following screenshot highlights the significant fields of a TCP header:

```
⊞ Frame 7: 674 bytes on wire (5392 bits), 674 bytes captured (5392 bits) on interface 0
⊞ Ethernet II, Src: HonHaiPr_99:db:85 (00:1c:25:99:db:85), Dst: CiscoCon_21:b7:ec (c8:d7:19:21:b7:ec)
⊞ Internet Protocol Version 4, Src: 192.168.1.116 (192.168.1.116), Dst: 162.159.241.165 (162.159.241.165)
⊟ Transmission Control Protocol, Src Port: 54579 (54579), Dst Port: http (80), Seq: 1, Ack: 1, Len: 616
    Source port: 54579 (54579)
    Destination port: http (80)
    [Stream index: 1]
    Sequence number: 1       (relative sequence number)
    [Next sequence number: 617      (relative sequence number)]
    Acknowledgment number: 1       (relative ack number)
    Header length: 20 bytes
  ⊞ Flags: 0x018 (PSH, ACK)
    Window size value: 16425
    [Calculated window size: 16425]
    [Window size scaling factor: -1 (unknown)]
  ⊞ Checksum: 0x58e8 [validation disabled]
  ⊞ [SEQ/ACK analysis]
  ⊞ [Timestamps]
⊞ Hypertext Transfer Protocol
```

Layer 5 – the session layer

The session layer handles setting up, controlling, and ending sessions within an application between two computers. This is not necessarily the same thing as, for example, a TCP connection, although the two will be related. The application sessions can span and outlive multiple network connections. An example of a networking protocol that operates at this layer is **Network Basic Input/Output System (NetBIOS)**.

Layer 6 – the presentation layer

The presentation layer converts incoming and outgoing data from one format to another and handles encryption/decryption and/or compression if any of these are required. The presentation layer is also responsible for the delivery and formatting of information to the application layer for further processing or display. An example of a presentation service would be the conversion of an EBCDIC-coded text computer file to an ASCII-coded file.

Layer 7 – the application layer

The application layer, which may (or may not) perform separate functions from the application itself, handles message formatting, human to machine interfaces, and so on. This layer represents the services that directly support applications such as software for file transfers, database access, e-mail, and so on.

In many widely used applications, no distinction is made between the presentation and application layers. For example, **HyperText Transfer Protocol (HTTP)**, which is generally regarded as an application-layer protocol, has presentation-layer aspects such as the ability to identify character encoding for proper conversion, which is then done in the application layer.

In the DARPA model, the OSI layers 5-7 are combined into an application layer. From a packet analysis standpoint, the particular manifestations and visibility (in Wireshark) of the functions in the top layer(s) will vary depending on the applications and specific protocols employed to support them.

The following diagram summarizes the OSI and DARPA layers and how various networking protocols and services align with these layers and each other:

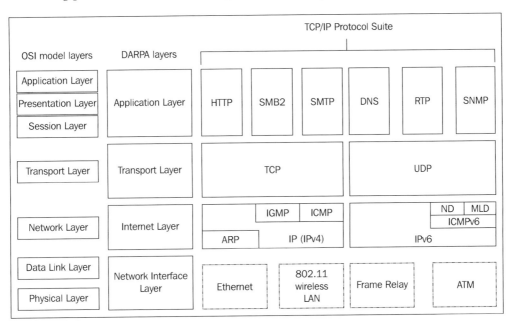

Encapsulation

You may have observed by now that packets encapsulate various protocols into successive layers, just like peeling an onion. An Ethernet frame contains a datagram payload; this datagram is a packet with an IP header and payload. The IP packet payload consists of a TCP header and data segment, which in turn may contain an HTTP header and payload. This encapsulation is easier to visualize when working within Wireshark's **Packet Details** pane.

IP networks and subnets

Before moving on, a short review of typical IP subnetting terms and typical applications should help clarify the terms used in this book and will act as a refresher for those already versed in IP addressing.

A /24 designator placed after a network IP address in diagrams or device configurations is a **Classless Inter-Domain Routing (CIDR)** designator that indicates the following:

- The first 24 out of the 32 bits in the 4-byte IP address represents the network portion of any IP address on this network. This network is designated as 10.1.1.0 (the next /24 network would be 10.1.2.0, then 10.1.3.0, and so on).

- The last 8 bits of the 32-bit address can be used to give workstations, hosts, and other devices an IP address, with the following exceptions:
  - The first host address on this network is reserved as a network designator to build routing tables: 10.1.1.0 (typically called the loopback address)
  - The last *host* address on this network is reserved as an IP broadcast address: 10.1.1.255

  The 8 bits binary is equal to 256 decimal, minus the preceding two exceptions. This leaves 254 usable IP addresses for devices, starting with 10.1.1.1, 10.1.1.2, and so on up to 10.1.1.254.

- Another way of expressing subnet masks is in a dotted decimal format, 255.255.255.0, which again indicates that the first 24 bits of an IP address is the network and the remaining 8 bits are for hosts.

- There are Class A, Class B, and Class C address ranges, as well as a subset of IP ranges reserved as private addresses to use within organizations.

  The following table shows the IP address ranges in the three major classes:

Class of IP address	Starting IP address	Ending IP address
A	1.0.0.0	126.255.255.255
B	128.0.0.0	191.255.255.255
C	192.0.0.0	223.255.255.255

The following table shows the private IP address ranges:

Class of private IP addresses	Starting IP address	Ending IP address
A	10.0.0.0	10.255.255.255
B	172.16.0.0	172.32.255.255
C	192.168.0.0	192.168.255.255

- Subnet masks can be configured to allow more or fewer hosts per subnet with a corresponding tradeoff in having fewer or greater network addresses with which to build multiple networks within larger organizations.

A deeper review of IP addressing and subnetting is beyond the scope of this book. If you're not familiar with these concepts, some additional study would be advisable as a solid understanding of IP subnetting is essential for most analysis activities.

Switching and routing packets

So far, we've covered the topics required to discuss how packets of data get routed from computer A to host B across LANs and/or WANs over distances that may range from across a room to across the globe. The important concepts to remember are that Ethernet frames work with switches and IP packets work with routers to accomplish this feat, which we'll cover in the next section.

Ethernet frames and switches

To reiterate what was outlined in the layer 2 (the data-link layer) discussion, Ethernet frames are switched from the entry port to the appropriate destination port based on the destination MAC address. Network switches build tables of which MAC addresses belong to each port, compare a frame's destination MAC address to these tables, and switch the frame to the appropriate egress port if the destination is on the same switch or out a trunk port to another switch or router otherwise.

Note that the first time a switch sees a destination MAC address it doesn't recognize, it sends the packet (which will usually be an ARP packet) out all the ports until a device answers and it can add the new MAC address to its **content addressable memory (CAM)** table that maps MAC addresses to specific ports.

Frames carrying packets destined for remote networks are sent to the default gateway port MAC address. If you look at a list of MAC addresses in the **Ethernet** tab of a **Conversations** table in Wireshark and see an address with a drastically higher volume of traffic than the other stations, this is likely a default gateway (router) port MAC address. This port is the pathway into/out of this LAN from/to other networks.

On any given LAN, you'll see workstations, servers, and routers generating ARP and **Domain Name Service (DNS)** requests:

- **ARP**: This is used to resolve IP addresses to MAC addresses
- **DNS**: This is used to resolve hostnames to IP addresses

In the following diagram, there are two user workstations and a server that are connected together in a LAN residing on the `10.1.1.0/24` IP network. A router is attached to this network, which has a WAN link to another location.

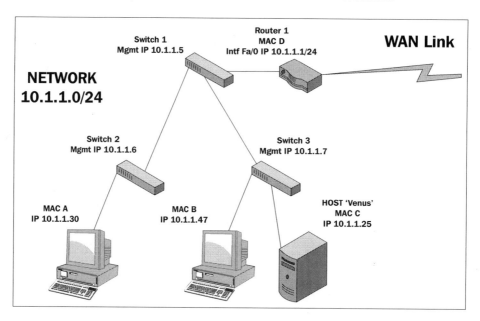

The following two scenarios leverage this drawing to show how MAC addresses are utilized to switch Ethernet frames around local area networks:

- The workstation with MAC address B wants to use an application on the server Venus, which is unknown to all the network devices as it was just powered up. The workstation knows the IP address of Venus as the IP address was preconfigured in the client application, but it doesn't know the server's MAC address.

The workstation broadcasts an ARP packet with its own MAC and IP address as the sender, the IP address of the Venus server, and all the zeros for the MAC address in the **Target** fields. Venus responds to the workstation with an ARP response that includes its MAC address of C in the sender MAC address.

The workstation then sends a session initiation packet to the server using the server's MAC address as the destination MAC in the Ethernet frame.

These Ethernet frames traversed switch 3, which learned both devices' MAC addresses from observing the ARP conversations. The rest of the switches in the LAN network learned workstation C's MAC address when it broadcasted its ARP packet (because switch 3 sent this ARP packet out all ports), but not the server's MAC as the server responded directly to C.

- The workstation with MAC address A now wants to use an application on the server Venus. It doesn't know the server's MAC address either, so it sends an ARP request as well, which switch 2 broadcasts out all its ports, as does switch 1 and switch 3 as the switches only look at MAC addresses and the destination MAC address of any ARP request is **ff:ff:ff:ff:ff:ff**, so each switch is obliged to send the broadcast frame out all ports.

However, when the server Venus responds to A's ARP packet, using A's MAC address, each switch in the path has learned which ports it saw A's MAC address come in on. So, each switch only sends Venus' response out the appropriate port back to workstation A. The same is true for learned non-broadcast frames. If a switch doesn't recognize a destination MAC address of a nonbroadcast frame, these are sent out all ports the first time as well.

As switch CAM tables get populated with MAC addresses and their associated ports, the number of frames that must be sent to every device in the LAN as well as the workload on all these devices is reduced significantly.

IP addresses and routers

When packets need to leave the LAN to get to a remote IP network, routers are required to route the packets based on their destination IP addresses. The following scenario (still referring to the preceding screenshot) illustrates some of the details involved in one possible situation.

Workstation A now wants to use an application on the server Mars, which resides on a different network than in the previous scenarios. And in this case, workstation A doesn't know the IP address of the server; it only needs its name. Workstation A will send a DNS request packet to the DNS server IP address configured in its network settings (the DNS server isn't shown here) with the hostname Mars; the DNS server will return the IP address of Mars 10.1.2.25. Workstation A calculates that this host isn't on its own network from a comparison of its IP address and subnet mask with Mars' IP address, so it sends the session initiation packet to router 1, which was configured as its default gateway in its network settings. We'll assume that Workstation A already knows the MAC address of router 1's port from a previous ARP exchange to find router 1's MAC address from the given IP address.

When the router receives A's frame, which was sent to the router port's MAC address, it inspects the destination IP address inside the IP header and looks up the appropriate port to forward the packet to. This routing process is supported by routing table entries the router builds from route information broadcasted by other routers; each router tells all the others what networks it knows a route to.

In this case, the Ethernet frame surrounding A's packet is stripped off and the remaining payload (packet) is sent across the WAN link to router 2, which also inspects the IP header destination IP address and looks up the correct port to forward the packet to. Router 2 wraps the packet in a new Ethernet frame with its own MAC address X as the source and the Mars server's Y address as the destination MAC (assuming the router already has the server in its MAC table), and transmits the packet out onto the LAN to get switched to the Mars server, as shown in the following diagram:

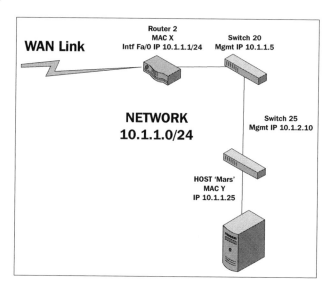

WAN links

Actually, network packets may traverse several routers and WAN links to reach the destination network, and each router traversed is called a hop. In the context of packet analysis, you should be aware that WAN links can introduce packet delivery delays or latency due to the following four major factors:

- **Physical speed-of-light propagation delay**: This is the amount of time required for electrical or light signals to travel across copper/fiber cables over long distances.

- **Network routing/geographical distance**: The WAN link routes are never in a straight line between points. They have to traverse major telephony switching centers and route along railways, roads, and other opportunistic paths.

- **Serialization delay into and across WAN links**: The WAN links are often slower speed links, and it takes a finite amount of time to send packet data across these links one bit at a time.

- **Queuing delays**: In network device buffers, including additional delays that may be induced by Quality of Service policies, some packets receive priority and others have to wait longer for their turn to be transmitted.

The effects of network delay incurred across LAN and WAN links can be seen and measured in Wireshark packet traces by inspecting the elapsed times between session setup packets.

Wireless networking

Wireless networks utilize a range of 802.11 specifications to provide connectivity over 2.4 or 5 GHz frequency bands at a variety of speeds. The significant differences between wireless frames and those found on wired networks are as follows:

- Wireless networks employ carrier sense (every station is listening), multiple access (shared medium), and collision avoidance (avoiding collisions instead of just recovering from them) techniques, which reduce the throughput

- In addition to data frames, which get forwarded to the wired network, wireless frame types include the following:

    ◦ **Management frames**: This is used for authentication and association tasks

    ◦ **Control frames**: This controls send/receive functions on the shared media to help avoid collisions

Wireshark can be used to capture and analyze packets on Wireless networks. However, in order to analyze the control and management frames, as well as select the radio channels to capture on without having to associate with a specific channel, specialized adapters are required. These adapters are available from various networking vendors.

These wireless adapters and their drivers enable Wireshark to display a pseudo header just below the frame header in the **Packet Details** pane, which includes information about:

- **Data rate**: This is the maximum data transfer rate possible across the radio channel

- **Channel frequency**: This is the RF channel frequency that the station is using

- **Channel type**: This is the 802.11 protocol used, and the common types are *a*, *b*, *g*, and *n*

- **RF signal and noise levels**: This is the received RF signal strength and background noise levels; the larger the difference between these two the better the signal can be decoded

Remember when analyzing wireless networks, the wireless access points utilize a wired LAN connection to the rest of the network that may warrant a separate analysis. The access point strips off the 802.11 header and encapsulates a packet in an Ethernet frame before sending the packet off on the wired network.

The following screenshot illustrates the contents of a typical **Radiotap Header** and **IEEE 802.11 frame**; note the **Data Rate**, **Channel frequency**, and **Signal/Noise** values:

```
Frame 1138: 2174 bytes on wire (17392 bits), 2174 bytes captured (17392 bits) on interface 0
Radiotap Header v0, Length 26
    Header revision: 0
    Header pad: 0
    Header length: 26
  Present flags
    MAC timestamp: 664141796
  Flags: 0x50
    Data Rate: 12.0 Mb/s
    Channel frequency: 2437 [BG 6]
  Channel type: 802.11g (pure-g) (0x00c0)
    SSI Signal: -72 dBm
    SSI Noise: -86 dBm
    Antenna: 0
    SSI Signal: 14 dB
IEEE 802.11 Unrecognized (Reserved frame), Flags: .p.P.....
    Type/Subtype: Unknown (0x2d)
  Frame Control Field: 0xd850
    .100 0010 1110 1100 = Duration: 17132 microseconds
    Receiver address: 0f:14:3e:76:25:1e (0f:14:3e:76:25:1e)
    Destination address: 0f:14:3e:76:25:1e (0f:14:3e:76:25:1e)
    Transmitter address: 49:f1:33:a5:c7:84 (49:f1:33:a5:c7:84)
    Source address: 49:f1:33:a5:c7:84 (49:f1:33:a5:c7:84)
    BSS Id: 6b:05:45:d9:c8:95 (6b:05:45:d9:c8:95)
    Fragment number: 13
    Sequence number: 3176
  Frame check sequence: 0x758f0b90 [incorrect, should be 0x0992caf1]
  Qos Control: 0x0e14
```

There are numerous reference materials and books that you can read to learn more about networking and network protocols. One of the classic sources is *TCP/IP Illustrated Volumes I, II, and III, W. Richard Stevens, Addison-Wesley Professional*, available online or in book formats.

Summary

The important points covered in this chapter included how Ethernet frames are switched to the appropriate switch ports on a LAN based on destination MAC addresses that packets are routed across and to remote networks based on destination IP addresses, and how the frames carrying packets destined for remote networks based on the destination IP address are sent to the default gateway's port MAC address.

We also covered how and why slower and/or longer distance WAN links can add significant amounts of delay to packet transmissions, which slows application data exchanges and increases user response times. We finished the chapter by discussing how Wireshark can capture and analyze packets on 802.11 wireless networks using specialized adapters.

In the next chapter, we'll cover in detail how to capture and filter packets using Wireshark.

3
Capturing All the Right Packets

In order to analyze packets to troubleshoot connectivity, performance, or security issues, you have to successfully capture all of the right packets and then identify and filter out just the packets that pertain to the goal at hand.

In this chapter, we will cover the following topics:

- Picking the best capture point
- TAPs and switch port mirroring
- Wireshark's capture interfaces, filters, and options
- Verifying a good capture
- Isolating the conversation(s) of interest
- Using the Wireshark Conversations window
- Wireshark's display filters
- Filtering expression buttons
- Following TCP/UDP/SSL streams
- Marking and ignoring packets
- Saving filtered traffic

You'll recognize that many of these activities are the same ones that we accomplished in *Chapter 1, Getting Acquainted with Wireshark*, to perform a capture and filter just the packets involved in loading a web page. In this chapter, we'll expand and finish rounding out your skills in all these topics.

Picking the best capture point

Determining the best location to perform a packet capture depends on several considerations:

- The nature of the issue being investigated
- The relative ability to perform a capture in a location that provides the highest degree of usefulness to the analysis
- The amount of technical difficulty, risk, and time required to perform a capture at a given location

User location

If you're troubleshooting a user complaint, the first capture point should be at the user's workstation to gain a view from the user's perspective and verify/clarify the situation that the user is reporting. From this vantage point, you can:

- Ensure that basic network services such as ARP and DNS are working correctly
- Analyze the initial login process if the user authentication involves a different device than the target application server
- Measure network round trip times from the user to the target host(s)
- Determine whether the TCP session setup handshake is appropriate for the application being accessed
- Measure service response times (such as HTTP or SMB response times)
- Determine whether the user is experiencing packet loss and retransmissions, out-of-order packets, or other network-related anomalies
- Capture any application error messages being sent to the user and the requests that resulted in those errors

Capturing from a user's location is usually much simpler from a practical standpoint and there is a lot less traffic to deal with, which makes capture sizes smaller and filtering the packets of interest simpler. Disconnecting a user's Ethernet cable for a few minutes to insert a TAP (we'll discuss these in the next section) or installing Wireshark on the user's workstation does not typically require special authorization or preparation as the risk to other users is negligible.

Server location

If a capture from a complaining user's workstation isn't possible or practical, a capture from the server end can still be useful, but it might be advantageous to apply a capture filter to gather just the traffic to/from the user's workstation (based on the user's IP address) to limit the capture file size. You can still measure network round trip times, server response times, analyze TCP handshake details, and detect retransmissions caused by packet loss, and perhaps the login/authentication process from this location.

Capturing from a server location is also appropriate when analyzing backend service response times. For example, if users interact with an application server but that app server performs transactions with a backend database in order to fulfill user requests and if there are complaints of slow response times, then an analysis of application server-to-database server interactions can help isolate the true source of the poor performance to one or the other host and the types of requests that result in slow or erroneous responses.

Other capture locations

For the majority of packet captures, you'll likely be at user workstations or server switch ports, but there will also be some cases where captures will need to be performed at other locations.

Mid-network captures

Identifying the source of excessive packet loss or disordering over a network path may require performing packet captures at various points along that path, typically at distribution or core switch trunks, or interfaces to routers, firewalls, and so on, to find the network segment where packet loss becomes apparent.

Both sides of specialized network devices

Today's modern networks often employ a number of network devices that can actually alter the contents of packets flowing between clients and servers; in some (occasional or last resort) cases, it may be necessary to capture on both sides of these devices to isolate or prove a functional or configuration problem:

- **Routers and gateways**: These are also called Internet gateways in some configurations and may be configured to perform a **Network Address Translation (NAT)** function that alters and hides the user's actual IP address from an outside network. This is done by substituting a public IP address for the user's real address. This usually involves translating port numbers as well so that a single public IP address can be used to support multiple sessions; in which case, the solution is called **Port Address Translation (PAT)**. The end result of the PAT functionality is that a capture from the client side and a capture at the server side of the same session conversation will involve different IP addresses and port numbers.

  The following diagram illustrates how a PAT device translates IP addresses and ports from an internal private network to and from an externally visible IP address and has translated the ports used for an individual user session:

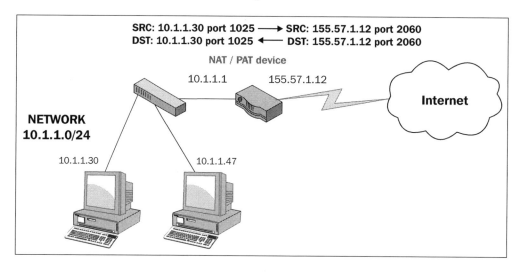

- **Proxy servers and firewalls**: Devices such as these can act as an intermediary between clients wanting to use resources from other (usually external) servers. These devices are most typically deployed between users inside a company and outside (web) services accessed via the Internet. These devices are employed for their security capabilities, allowing administrative control over what can be accessed and the type of data content that can be relayed between the two networks, malware scanning, and so on. From a packet analysis standpoint, you should be aware that in addition to performing a NAT/PAT function, some implementations of these devices may actually terminate a user session on one side and initiate a completely different session between the device and the outside host on the other side, on behalf of the user, such that the TCP handshake and session parameters, IP addresses and port numbers, and packet sizes can all differ on either side.

- **IP tunnels using Generic Routing Encapsulation**: These are used to connect two IP networks that don't otherwise have a native routing path to each other. The original packets are encapsulated inside packets with different IP addresses appropriate for the network media that they will traverse. The most common use of IP tunneling is to connect private corporate networks together through public Internet connections or to connect **Internet Protocol Version 6 (IPv6)** networks together over traditional IPv4 network paths. IP tunnels can be configured between routers and high-end switches.

Although it may be necessary (to validate an issue to other support teams) or more practical to capture at or near the interfaces to the devices described earlier, it is usually easier and just as effective to perform the captures at user and/or server locations. Unless you're part of a network support team, you won't have to conduct an analysis in such an advanced and complicated environment.

Test Access Ports and switch port mirroring

If you're capturing from a user location and cannot or do not wish to install Wireshark on the user's machine or you're capturing at another location in the network, you have two options to obtain a copy of the packets traversing the network: Test Access Ports or switch port mirroring.

Test Access Port

A **Test Access Port** (**TAP**) is a device that copies all the packets flowing through it to one or more monitor ports. A station with Wireshark installed on it can be connected to one of the monitor ports to capture the packets.

You should select an aggregating TAP that supports the link speed of the network ports being analyzed (usually 100 Mbps or 1 Gbps) and that will copy and combine the packets flowing in both directions (transmit data from the user's workstation and receive data from the network); the aggregating TAP funnels the traffic to a single connection (transmit to the Wireshark station) so that you can capture the traffic in both directions with a single network interface on the Wireshark station. Be aware that since you're copying packets from two directions into one pipe to the Wireshark station, it is possible to oversubscribe the monitor port if traffic rates are extremely high. If this happens, the excess packets will be dropped. Oversubscription usually isn't a concern at user workstations, but it could be for switch trunks or other high traffic areas.

The following figure illustrates how a TAP is inserted between a user workstation and that workstation's switch port, and how a Wireshark workstation is attached to capture packets:

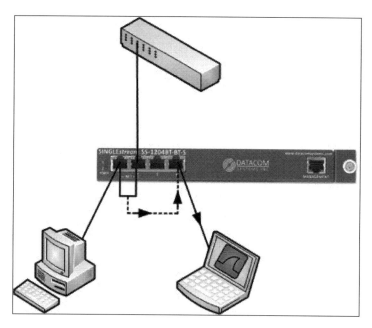

Switch port mirroring

Switch port mirroring, also known as a **Switched Port Analyzer (SPAN)** feature or spanning a port, is the practice of configuring a network switch to perform the same function as a TAP: to make a copy of the packets flowing in and out of a specified port and send them to an otherwise unused monitor port where a Wireshark station is attached to capture the packets.

The advantage of using port mirroring is that no connections need to be broken to insert a TAP. The monitor port can be easily configured by a switch administrator and just as easily disabled.

The potential issues with this option include the fact that not all switches support port mirroring, and there is some evidence to suggest that using this feature can affect the performance of the switch, at least for the port being monitored. The possibility of oversubscribing the monitor port from excessive transmit plus receiving traffic levels also exists for port mirroring, as is the case when using a TAP, and this is likely when monitoring switch trunks to other switches, as these will be carrying traffic for multiple users.

The following diagram is a simple illustration of a port mirroring scenario on a switch. The packets to and from the workstation port are copied to the port where the Wireshark station is connected.

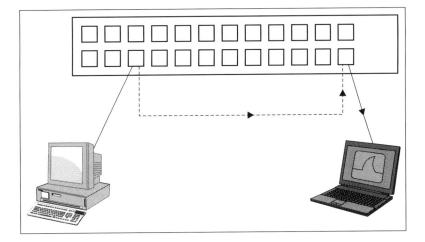

Capturing packets on high traffic rate links

If you need to capture packets on a high traffic rate link such as a trunk link between larger switches, Wireshark is probably not the best solution. It may not be able to keep up with a busy link. Wireshark is actually a GUI tool that calls a command-line executable called **dumpcap**, which captures the packets and saves them to a disk file. Wireshark reads this file and presents the processed packets to the user interface. An alternative to Wireshark is to use the dumpcap or **tcpdump** executable directly (these are covered in *Chapter 8, Command-line and Other Utilities*) or a high performance capture appliance offered by numerous vendors.

Capturing interfaces, filters, and options

Capturing packets with Wireshark consists of selecting the correct network interface to capture packets from, applying any capture filters that may be appropriate, and applying the correct options to accomplish the capture in the desired manner. We'll cover these three topics in the following sections.

Selecting the correct network interface

As discussed in *Chapter 1, Getting Acquainted with Wireshark*, if you have multiple network interfaces on your machine, you need to determine and select the correct interface to capture packets. In Wireshark's **Capture** menu, click on **Interface** or click on the first icon on the icon bar.

The **Wireshark Capture Interfaces** window provides a list and description of the network interfaces on your machine, the IP addresses assigned, and the total packets and packets per second counters for each interface. If an interface has an IPv6 address assigned and this is being displayed, you can click on the address to toggle and display the IPv4 address.

The following screenshot illustrates a typical **Capture Interfaces** window listing a LAN and wireless interface along with their IP addresses and packet counters:

The **Capture Interfaces** window provides the following two options:

- Clicking on the **Details** button for any of the listed interfaces opens an **Interface Details** window that provides a wide range of information that can be useful to verify the interface's operation. The status of the **Link** and **Link Speed** information is displayed in the **Characteristics** tab, and the MAC address of the selected NIC is displayed in the **802.3 (Ethernet)** tab.

- The rest of the capture options are configured in the **Capture Options** window, which is opened by clicking on the **Options** button in the **Capture Interfaces** window, or by selecting **Options** from the **Capture** menu, or by clicking on the second icon in the icon bar.

The following screenshot illustrates a typical **Capture Options** window with a number of options specified. You can refer to it for examples of the topics on **Capture Options**.

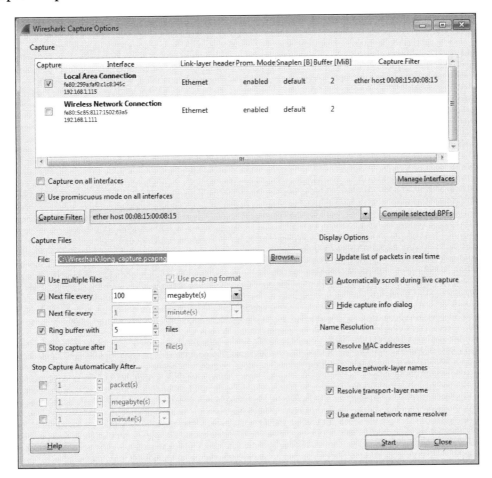

As seen in the preceding screenshot, the **Capture Options** window displays the available interfaces and their IP addresses and allows you to select one or more of these interfaces to perform the capture. Wireshark can capture from multiple interfaces simultaneously, as well as from virtual interfaces. The primary advantage of starting with the **Capture Interfaces** window is the availability of the packet counters to aid in identifying active interfaces, a feature not available in the **Capture Options** window. Otherwise, if you know which interface you'll want to use, you can skip using the **Capture Interfaces** window and start here.

Clicking on the **Manage Interfaces** button in the **Capture Options** window brings up an **Interface Management** window. From the **Local Interfaces** tab, you can select to hide interfaces that you do not wish to see displayed in the **Capture Interfaces** and **Capture Options** windows.

There is an option to quickly enable **Capture on all interfaces** and a **Use promiscuous mode on all interfaces** option that is enabled by default. In most cases, this option should be left enabled so that the chosen interface(s) can capture and save all the packets seen. Otherwise, only the packets that are being sent to the Wireshark workstation's MAC address, broadcast, and/or multicast packets will be seen and captured, which basically negates its usefulness as a capture device. The **Compile selected BPFs** button provides a machine language display of the compiled capture filter, but has no other functional purpose.

> The **Capture Filter** field has a highlighting feature that indicates valid versus invalid filter syntax. A green background indicates a good filter and a red background indicates an invalid or incomplete filter.

Using capture filters

Capture filters are used to reduce the amount of traffic saved during a packet capture. In practice, capture filters should be used sparingly, if used at all, to help make sure that no packets that are important for an analysis are inadvertently missed because they fall outside the capture filter parameters. Remember that you can always filter out unwanted traffic from a capture, but you can't do anything about missed packets once the capture is finished. If you're unsure about a capture, perform the capture again with a more generous capture filter or none at all.

One scenario where a capture filter is appropriate is when you want to let a capture run for a long period of time. Then, you should filter out as much extraneous traffic as possible to keep capture file sizes under control. However, take care to make sure the capture filter you apply doesn't exclude any traffic that may be useful for the analysis.

It's usually a good idea to do some trial captures when using capture filters to verify that the filter is working as desired before doing the official capture that you want to keep.

Configuring capture filters

Wireshark provides a **Capture Filter** window that makes it easy to select a preconfigured capture filter, or you can configure your own based on your needs.

Click on the **Capture Filter** button in the **Capture Options** window to open the **Capture Filters** window. From this window, you can select from a number of useful preconfigured capture filters, create a new and unique capture filter for your purposes, or delete unwanted or erroneous filters. Creating a new filter only involves giving the filter a name, entering the capture filter syntax, clicking on **New** to save the filter, and then finally clicking on **OK**. Alternatively, you can click on an existing filter and then click on **New**, which will create a copy of that filter at the bottom of the list that can then be modified for your purposes.

The following screenshot illustrates a typical **Capture Filter** window. In this case, a capture filter that will only allow traffic to and from a specific Ethernet MAC address has been selected:

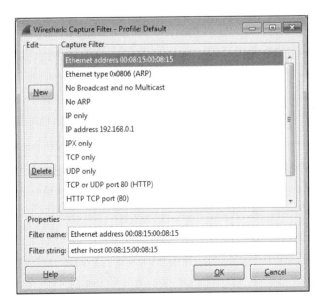

Wireshark's capture filters use a syntax that is known as the **Berkley Packet Filter (BPF)** format, which has legacy roots in the Unix world and is still in use today with packet-level drivers. Note that the syntax used to capture filters in Wireshark differs significantly from the syntax used for display filters.

The default selection of capture filters from the **Capture Filter** window is helpful in providing examples of capture filter syntax. Some additional examples of capture filter syntax and examples of that syntax are outlined in the following table:

Description	Syntax	Examples
Filter on an Ethernet MAC address	`ether host xx:xx:xx:xx:xx:xx`	`ether host 00:1c:25:99:db:85`
Filter to capture just the traffic from or to a MAC address	`ether src` or `ether dst`	`ether src 00:1c:25:99:db:85`
Filter on an IP address or hostname	`host xxx.xxx.xxx.xxx`	`host 192.168.1.115` `host www.wireshark.org`
Filter to capture just the traffic between two IP addresses		`host 192.168.1.115 and host 10.1.1.125`
Filter traffic in one direction only between two hosts	`src host and dst host`	`src host 192.168.1.115 and dst host 10.1.1.125`
Filter based on a port number	`port, dst port,` and `src port`	
Filter for DNS packets		`port 53`
Filter for DHCP packets		`port 67`
Filter based on a protocol	`arp, icmp, ip, upd, tcp, http, ip6,` and `icmp6`	
Filter for HTTP traffic only		`http`
Capture filter logical operators	`=, !=, >, <, >=, <=, !, not, &&, and, ||, or`	
Filter to exclude ARP and DNS packets		`not arp and port not 53` `! arp && port ! 53`

More information and examples of capture filters can be found on the Wireshark wiki at `http://wiki.wireshark.org/CaptureFilters` and the protocol-specific capture filter syntax is included in the reference information found at `http://wiki.wireshark.org/ProtocolReference`.

Capture options

The Wireshark **Capture Options** window offers a variety of controls to configure captures to suit a particular need.

Capturing filenames and locations

Clicking on the **Browse** button on the **File** option allows you to navigate to a chosen directory in which you can store the capture files and enter a filename for the capture files.

When the **File** option is used, Wireshark will append a file number and date-time stamp to the filename you specify and will not provide a file extension. You should specify a `.pcapng` extension in the filename. This is better illustrated with an example.

The user provided directory and filename is `C:\Wireshark\long_capture.pcapng`, and Wireshark will create and save packets to files in the format `C:\Wireshark\long_capture_00001_20140724132952.pcapng`.

If Wireshark is configured to capture to more than one file (this will be discussed later), the file numbers and date-time stamps will be incremented accordingly as the capture progresses, for example, `long_capture_00002_20140724133343.pcapng` and `long_capture_00003_20140724133612.pcapng`.

Multiple file options

Wireshark can be configured to save packets to multiple files to allow long-term captures, and offers a number of options to control how this is accomplished.

Selecting the **Use multiple files** option causes the appropriate underlying controls to become active as specific options are enabled. You can choose to start a new (next) file when each file reaches a given size and/or after a configurable period.

 Wireshark can become very sluggish or might even crash when working with capture file sizes of much greater than 100 MB, so you should consider this as a good maximum file size.

Ring buffer

The **Ring buffer** option works in conjunction with the **Next File every** option to cause Wireshark to fill the specified number of files, and as the capture continues to progress, it deletes the oldest files.

This feature is useful to keep a capture running while waiting for some intermittent problem or an event to occur, after which the capture is manually stopped. The ring buffer files provide historical capture data for a period just prior to stopping the capture, without filling a hard drive with an excessive number of large capture files.

Stop capture options

Wireshark has options to automatically stop a capture after a specified number of packets, file size, or time period. If the **Use multiple files** option is enabled, an option to stop the capture after a specified number of files can be employed. Otherwise, the capture can be stopped after a specified number of packets, file size, or time period has elapsed.

Display options

The **Update list of packets in real time** option specifies that Wireshark is to periodically read the capture file as it is being written during the capture and update the **Packet List** contents accordingly. Otherwise, the Wireshark user interface will be grayed out during the capture.

The **Automatically scroll during live capture** option specifies that Wireshark updates and displays the latest captured packets in the **Packet List** pane such that the packets seem to scroll up as the list is updated. The **Update list of packets in real time** option must be enabled for this option to function.

Both of these options have a processing time cost that could result in lost packets and/or a sluggish display and should be disabled if capturing on a very busy link. However, the ability to view and confirm that the expected packet flows are occurring during the capture will be lost.

The **Hide capture info dialog** option (which is enabled by default) controls whether a simple window is displayed during the capture that displays the packet counts and percentages by protocol. Unless specifically needed, it is best to leave this window hidden.

Name resolution options

If the **Resolve MAC addresses** option is enabled, it causes Wireshark to display MAC addresses with an assigned manufacturer code in place of the first three octets. For example, Wireshark will display **CiscoCon_21:b7:ec** instead of **c8:d7:19:21:b7:ec**. The list of manufacturer's codes is kept in the `manuf` file of the Wireshark installation directory.

The **Resolve network-layer names** option works in conjunction with **Use external network name resolver** to determine if or how captured IP addresses are resolved into their hostnames, as follows:

- The **Resolve network-layer names** option specifies that Wireshark should attempt to resolve IP addresses into hostnames. If the **Use external network name resolver** option is enabled, Wireshark will perform reverse DNS lookups for each unique IP address. This causes Wireshark to generate traffic of its own.

- If the **Use external network name resolver** option is disabled, Wireshark will attempt to resolve the IP addresses using a `hosts` text file provided by a user (which uses typical IP address `<tab>` hostname syntax) located in the Wireshark installation directory when using a default profile or in the appropriate profile directory when using a custom profile.

During a capture, it is better to leave the **Resolve network-layer names** option disabled so that Wireshark isn't creating additional network traffic while trying to resolve IP addresses during a capture. This feature can always be temporarily enabled (by navigating to **View | Name Resolution | Enable for network layer** from the menu) after the capture is finished.

If the **Resolve transport-layer name** option is enabled, it causes Wireshark to display the human-readable, port- and protocol-specific services' names instead of the port numbers in the Info display field in the **Packet List** pane. For example, TCP port 80 will be displayed as HTTP. The list of port number services is kept in the `services` file in the Wireshark installation directory.

The screenshot at the beginning of this section illustrates a **Capture Option** window set to use the LAN interface, a filter to capture traffic only to and from a specific Ethernet MAC address, to save up to five files of 100 MB each in a ring buffer scenario, and to save those files in a provided directory with a specific leading filename and extension. The **Display Options** and **Name Resolution** options have been left in their default settings.

Once all the desired **Capture Options** have been selected, clicking on the **Start** button will start the capture.

Having covered all the most useful **Capture Options** features, now is probably the right time to tell you that for many of your captures, especially from a relatively low traffic volume location such as from a user workstation, you don't want or need to set any capture options (except the appropriate interface to capture from) and can simply jump into starting a capture using all the defaults by clicking on the third (green shark-fin shaped) icon on the icon bar or selecting **Start** from the **Capture** menu. Not using a capture filter allows you to capture all the relevant packets—without missing anything—and filter any unwanted traffic out using display filters after the capture is done.

Verifying a good capture

After a capture is complete, you should scroll through and inspect the packets in the **Packet List** pane to ensure that you're seeing the traffic you were expecting—usually traffic to and from a specific host.

You should also ensure there were no dropped packets, which would be displayed in the **Packet Information** section of the **Status Bar** at the bottom center of the Wireshark user interface. Dropped packets indicate that Wireshark or the selected NIC could not keep up with the traffic volume and had to discard packets, which could of course affect the quality of your analysis. If dropped packets occur, you may need to use a higher performance workstation to perform the captures or select a lower traffic volume capture location.

Saving the bulk capture file

After completing and verifying a good capture, you should save the bulk (all captured packets) capture file (assuming a single file capture) to your directory of choice. You will later be filtering and saving a subset of packets to a smaller file, but it is advantageous to be able to load the original capture file again at a later time if during the analysis you discover that you might have inadvertently filtered out more packets than you wanted.

Using the **Save As** option in the **File** menu, navigate to the directory of your choice and give the file a name. If no file extension is specified, Wireshark will append a file extension based on the **Save as type** option selected; the default is the `.pcapng` format. However, you can save the file in several other popular vendor-specific formats if you intend to share the capture file with someone who is using a different protocol analysis tool.

If multiple files were saved using one of the multiple file and/or ring buffer capture options, navigate to the **File | File Set | List Files** to select and open one of the files.

Isolating conversations of interest

After you have completed a packet capture and saved a bulk capture file, you'll be with an almost overwhelming number of packets of various types and addresses in the **Packet List** pane. It's now time to par this down to just the packets that pertain to the analysis task at hand.

The idea is to progressively eliminate unrelated packets; analyze the pertinent conversations looking for anomalies; and again progressively filter, measure, and analyze packet flow and application behavior until you have discovered and can document the root cause of the issue.

There are two basic ways to isolate and inspect packets and conversations of interest, and you'll likely use both of the following methods in most of your analysis activities:

- **Conversations**: This window creates a list of conversation pairs by MAC or IP address and/or TCP/UDP ports that can be sorted. It displays filters that will isolate and display only the selected conversation packets can be quickly applied from this window.
- **Display Filters**: These filters are based on MAC or IP addresses and/or protocol-specific fields that limit the packets displayed in the **Packet List** pane.

We'll discuss each of these methods in the following sections.

Using the Conversations window

The basics of using the **Conversations** window were covered during the first capture in *Chapter 1*, *Getting Acquainted with Wireshark*. In this section, we'll cover a few other handy features of the **Conversations** window.

The Ethernet tab

The **Conversations** window exhibits specific behaviors in the **Ethernet** tab, depending on the available **Name Resolution** settings. If **Enable for Network Layer** in the **Name Resolution** menu, which can be found in the **View** menu, is enabled and **Name Resolution** is also enabled in the **Conversations** window, then the IP address that is associated with a given device's MAC address is displayed as an IP address instead of a MAC address. Toggling the **Name Resolution** option in this scenario is useful for easily associating a devices' IP address with its MAC address.

If the **Enable for Network Layer** option is not enabled, then the **Name Resolution** option in the **Conversations** window controls whether the MAC addresses are displayed with manufacturer prefixes or as the basic 6-octet MAC address.

The TCP and UDP tabs

The **TCP** and **UDP** tabs of the **Conversations** window list all of the conversations between devices based on IP addresses and ports. Considering that network communications between a pair of devices, each with their associated IP addresses, could include multiple sequential or simultaneous sessions with differing port numbers, the **TCP** and **UDP** tabs (depending on the protocol in use) make it much easier to inspect the number and relative size and start/duration of these individual sessions.

As can be done in any of the other tabs in the **Conversations** window, a display filter can be quickly prepared or applied using the right-click functionality.

A helpful practice when investigating TCP or UDP sessions is to apply a display filter on just the IP addresses initially and then enabling the **Limit to display filter** option at the bottom of the **Conversations** window. Upon returning to the **TCP** or **UDP** tab, only the port-level sessions between the filtered host pair are displayed, which makes investigating these sessions much easier than picking them out from the entire list.

The following screenshot shows the multiple TCP sessions that were involved in loading the `https://www.wireshark.org/` home page after applying a display filter (from the bulk capture file) and enabling the **Limit to display filter** option in the **Conversations** window. It can be seen that the (top) conversation between port **54581** on the user workstation and port 80 (HTTP) carried the vast majority of the traffic; the remaining ports carried much smaller amounts of traffic.

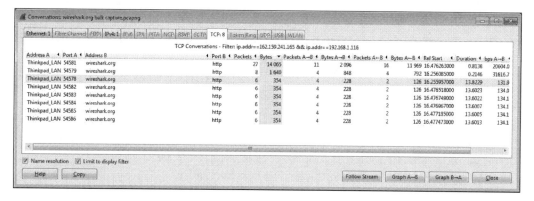

The WLAN tab

Since the **Conversations** window tabs are ordered alphabetically, the **WLAN** tab comes at the end. This tab displays the wireless station MAC addresses, as well as the **Bytes**, **Packets**, and other columns offered in the other tabs.

Wireshark display filters

Wireshark provides a very wide range of protocol-specific display filters that can be extremely useful for analysis activities by allowing you to focus on specific packets, based on criteria that you define. You can filter on just the traffic that you want to see or filter undesired traffic out of view. Display filters are one of the most helpful features of Wireshark, so they warrant becoming very familiar with.

Display filters can be created in several ways:

- By applying display filters from the **Display Filter** window
- By typing in the display filter syntax (using autocomplete)
- By applying display filters from the **Conversations** (or **Endpoints**) window
- By applying saved display filters from Filter Expression Buttons
- Using the **Expressions** button for assistance creating filters
- Using right-click menus on specific packet fields

 Remember that display filters use a proprietary Wireshark filter format, which is protocol-dependent and significantly different from capture filter syntax.

The Display Filter window

You can open the **Display Filter** window by selecting **Display Filters** from the **Analyze** menu, by clicking on the **Edit/apply display filter** icon on the icon bar, or by just clicking the **Filters** button next to the display filter textbox on the display filter bar.

The **Display Filter** window looks and functions in a similar fashion to the capture filters window, as shown in the following screenshot. You can create a new custom display filter to be added to this window by entering a filter name and the appropriate syntax and clicking on **New** or clicking an existing filter. Click on **New** and modify/rename as per your requirements.

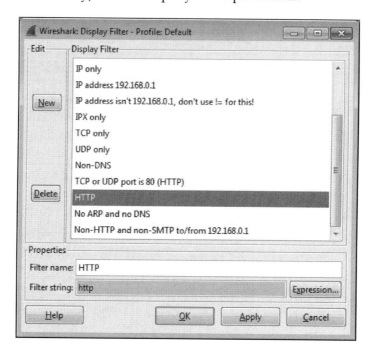

Display filters listed in this window were saved in a `dfilters` file in the Wireshark installation directory for the default profile and in the appropriate **Personal configuration** directory when custom profiles are in use.

When you apply a display filter, the **Status Bar** at the bottom of the Wireshark user interface screen reflects the total number of packets and the packets displayed, as illustrated in the following screenshot:

Packets: 423 · Displayed: 71 (16.8%) · Load time: 0:00.030

The display filter syntax

The default selection of capture filters from the **Display Filter** window shown previously provides examples of basic capture filter syntax. Additional examples of display filter syntax are outlined in the following table:

Description	Syntax	Examples
Basic protocols	arp, bootp, dns, dhcp6, eth, snmp, smb, smb2, icmp, rtp, ip, ipv6, udp, tcp, http, and sip	Same as syntax examples
Display filter comparison operators	eq, ==, ne, !=, gt, >, lt, <, ge, >=, le, <=, !, not, and, &&, or, ||, XOR, and ^^	ip.addr == 192.168.1.115 and !(ip.addr == 192.168.1.125)
Protocol-specific extensions	protocol-specific	ip.addr, tcp.port, tcp.dstport, tcp.analysis, udp.port, and udp.srcport
Classless InterDomain Routing (CIDR) notation on IPv4 addresses	A.B.C.D/CIDR notation	ip.addr == 192.168.1.0/24 that matches any IP address in the 192.168.1.0 subnet

Using the != operator on expressions such as eth.addr, ip.addr, tcp.port, and udp.port and alike may not work as expected as there are usually two addresses and ports in a packet, and the ! operator will not match both instances.

Use !(ip.addr == x.x.x.x) or a similar syntax for these types of filters.

More information and examples of display filters can be found on the Wireshark wiki at http://wiki.wireshark.org/DisplayFilters and protocol-specific display filter syntax is included in the reference information found at http://wiki.wireshark.org/ProtocolReference.

Typing in a display filter

You can type a display filter syntax directly into the **Filter** textbox in the display filter bar, and then click on **Apply** to apply the filter or **Clear** to clear a filter and start over.

A helpful feature of typing the display filter syntax into the textbox is the autocomplete function. Upon typing a protocol and then a period (.), the textbox will display a list of available protocol-related extensions that can be selected and then the appropriate comparison operator and value added before clicking on **Apply**.

The textbox also has a color-coded background indicating the display filter syntax status. If the syntax is incorrect or incomplete, the background is red and a correct filter results in a green background. A yellow background is a warning that the entered syntax may not work as expected.

Display filters from a Conversations or Endpoints window

Creating a display filter to be applied from a **Conversations** window has already been covered. The same functionality is available from an **Endpoints** window, which can be opened by selecting **Endpoint List** from the **Statistics** menu and one of the listed protocols.

Filter Expression Buttons

Filter Expression Buttons are buttons you can create that are based on display filters; these can be used to quickly apply previously-saved display filters to your capture data to identify network and application problems.

For example, to create a **Filter Expression Button** option that displays just **TCP SYN, SYN/ACK, FIN,** or **RST** packets to analyze the TCP session setup parameters, network round-trip delay times, and session terminations:

1. Type the following display filter string into the **Filter** textbox on the **Display Filter Bar**:

   ```
   (tcp.flags&02 && tcp.seq==0) || (tcp.flags&12 && tcp.seq==0) ||
   (tcp.flags.ack && tcp.seq==1 && !tcp.nxtseq > 0 && !tcp.ack >1)
   || tcp.flags.fin == 1 || tcp.flags.reset ==1
   ```

2. Clicking on **Apply** will apply this filter to a capture that you have loaded so that you can confirm that it is working properly.

3. Then, click on **Save** and give the button a name, such as TCP Handshake (as illustrated in the following screenshot). Then, click on **OK**:

The filter expression buttons you create will appear on the right-hand side of the initial controls in the display filter bar, as illustrated in the following screenshot:

The filter expression button definitions are stored in the preferences file for the profile you are using. You can edit the button display order, edit the name or filter syntax, or delete the buttons in Wireshark's Preferences window.

Using the Expressions window button

To the right-hand side of the textbox on the display filter toolbar is the **Expression** button. Clicking on this button opens a **Filter Expression** window that allows you to select a protocol and the extension to that protocol, one of the appropriate relation (comparison) operators, and assign a comparison value. Click on **OK** to populate the display filter textbox with the resultant display filter syntax and then click on **Apply** to apply the filter.

Right-click menus on specific packet fields

If you right-click on a specific field in the **Packet List** or **Packet Details** panes, you can select the **Apply as Filter** or **Prepare a Filter** option and the required submenu option to create display filter syntax, as illustrated in the following screenshot. This is a very quick way of creating display filter syntax:

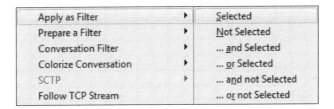

If you are selecting a field and using the right-click functionality to create display filter syntax, it is usually better to use the **Prepare a Filter** option, which will allow you to edit the syntax before clicking on **Apply** to apply the filter.

Clicking on a protocol field in the **Packet Details** pane results in that field and the display filter syntax that reflects that field to be displayed in the bottom-left **Status** bar field. This is very helpful for starting a display filter string that will use a particular field.

Following TCP/UDP/SSL streams

Selecting a packet in a conversation, right-clicking, and selecting a **Follow TCP Stream**, **Follow UDP Stream**, or **Follow SSL Stream** option (as appropriate) from the menu provides a display window that contains a textual depiction of the payload data from all of the packets in a conversation. This is an excellent way to inspect the contents of a stream without having to select and inspect multiple packets. Viewing the exchanges between the client and server can be very helpful for troubleshooting purposes.

When a **Follow** Stream option is selected for a given packet, a display filter is automatically created and applied to support creation of this window. The following screenshot illustrates a **Follow TCP Stream** window. Also, note the display filter syntax (**tcp.stream eq 15**) that was created and applied when this stream was selected:

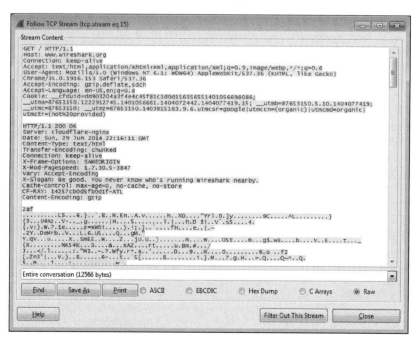

Marking and ignoring packets

You can toggle **Mark/Unmark Packet** or **Ignore/Unignore Packet** from the Wireshark **Edit** menu, or by right-clicking on a packet in the **Packet List** pane and selecting **Mark Packet (toggle)** or **Ignore Packet (toggle)**.

The menu displayed by right-clicking on a packet in the **Packet List** pane is shown in the following screenshot:

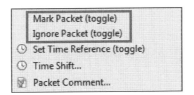

Wireshark allows you to mark one or more packets in the **Packet List** pane to make it easier to find those packets later by giving the packet entry a black background with white font. This marking can be toggled on and off on a per-packet basis. Marking a packet has no other effect on the display or packet context.

You can also ignore one or more packets. However, when you invoke the ignore function on a packet that packet entry disappears from the **Packet List**, **Packet Details**, and **Packet Bytes** panes and it effectively ceases (temporarily) to be part of the capture file. Note that ignoring packets can result in Wireshark reporting re-transmissions or other error conditions caused by the missing packet.

The ignored packets aren't actually deleted from the capture file as you can use the **Reload** option in the **View** menu or click the **Reload** icon on the icon bar to recover the ignored packets.

Saving the filtered traffic

During or after completing an analysis, you will want to save a set of filtered packets into a new capture file. Saving a filtered subset of the bulk capture data and opening the new, smaller file in Wireshark is helpful to reduce the distracting background noise packets displayed when clearing display filters, working with **Conversations** windows, and so on during your analysis. Finally, upon completing your analysis, you will want a filtered capture file that represents the analysis evidence and conclusion and can be quickly loaded for review at a later time.

Use the **Export Specified Packets** option in the **File** menu to save a new capture file consisting of just your filtered packets. Navigate to the desired directory; enter a filename (Wireshark will provide the appropriate filename extension); make the appropriate selections to save all the **Displayed** packets, **Marked packets**, and/or to **Remove Ignored packets**; and then click on **Save**. Remember to save the complete capture using the **Save As** option in the **File** menu as well, because you may need this file again.

The following screenshot illustrates a typical **Export Specified Packets** window and its selections:

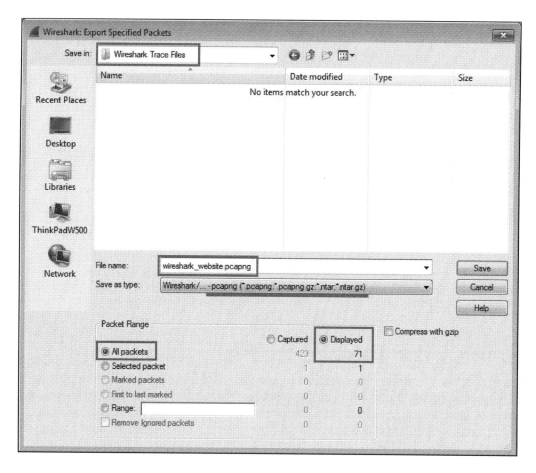

Summary

The important points covered in this chapter included picking an optimal capture point, selecting between TAPs and mirrored/SPAN ports, Wireshark's capture filters and options, verifying a good capture, using Wireshark's **Conversation** windows and display filters to isolate packets of interest, creating Filter Expression Buttons, marking and ignoring packets, and saving the filtered traffic for later or more detailed analysis.

In the next chapter, we'll cover the rest of Wireshark's basic packet analysis features.

4
Configuring Wireshark

Wireshark offers a number of features that can be configured to enhance
the accuracy and ease of performing packet analysis activities such as
troubleshooting a functional or performance problem. Selecting the best format
to measure the elapsed time between packets is an important factor. There are a
number of protocol-specific options that affect how Wireshark displays time-related
information that are useful as well. Coloring rules, preferences settings, and profiles
let you customize Wireshark for your particular style of analysis, as well as the
different environments that you might work in.

In this chapter, we will cover the following topics:

* Working with packet timestamps
* Colorization and coloring rules
* Wireshark preferences
* Wireshark profiles

These topics will wrap up our introduction to the most essential and useful features
and options of Wireshark.

Working with packet timestamps

Understanding how Wireshark handles time and using the right incarnation of
packet timestamp displays is crucial to properly analyze packet flows and identify
time-related anomalies.

How Wireshark saves timestamps

When packets are captured, Wireshark gives each packet a timestamp derived from the system clock of the machine from where the capture takes place. This timestamp is converted to **Universal Coordinated Time (UTC)** based on an offset calculated from the time zone setting and any **Daylight Savings Time (DST)** rules that apply for the capture machine, and then converted again to an epoch number (the UTC-based number of seconds since January 1, 1970). This is the time value that gets saved in the capture file for each packet. When Wireshark reads the capture file, it turns the epoch number back to the familiar date and time display, adjusted for the time zone and DST offsets for your machine.

This means that if a packet capture is conducted on a machine in Los Angeles, which has an offset from UTC of -8 hours, and you look at the same capture file on a machine in Berlin, which is UTC +1 hour (an overall difference of 9 hours, plus any DST differences), a packet that was captured at 10 a.m. local time in Los Angeles will display a timestamp of 7 p.m. in Berlin.

Examples of the timestamp displays in different time zones are shown in the following table:

	Los Angeles	London	Berlin	Bangalore
Capture file time (UTC)	10:00	10:00	10:00	10:00
Local offset to UTC	-8	0	+1	+5:30
Displayed time (local time)	02:00	10:00	11:00	17:30

If you're going to look at a packet capture someone has sent you and the absolute time when an event occurred is important to the analysis, you'll need to know or ask what time zone the capture was taken in, determine the offset between your time zone and the capture location time zone, and mentally make the time difference adjustment for the timestamps that Wireshark will display. Otherwise, this difference won't matter as you're usually more interested in the elapsed time or the time between specific events in the capture.

Wireshark time display options

There are a wide variety of packet time displays available for use in Wireshark. By default, Wireshark provides a **Time** column in the **Packet List** pane configured to display **Seconds Since Beginning of Capture** with microsecond resolution (123.123456) for each packet.

However, the way in which time is displayed in this column can be changed by selecting the desired format from the **Time Display Format** option in the **View** menu, which is illustrated in the following screenshot:

Date and Time of Day: 1970-01-01 01:02:03.123456	Ctrl+Alt+1
Time of Day: 01:02:03.123456	Ctrl+Alt+2
Seconds Since Epoch (1970-01-01): 1234567890.123456	Ctrl+Alt+3
• Seconds Since Beginning of Capture: 123.123456	Ctrl+Alt+4
Seconds Since Previous Captured Packet: 1.123456	Ctrl+Alt+5
Seconds Since Previous Displayed Packet: 1.123456	Ctrl+Alt+6
UTC Date and Time of Day: 1970-01-01 01:02:03.123456	Ctrl+Alt+7
UTC Time of Day: 01:02:03.123456	Ctrl+Alt+7
Automatic (File Format Precision)	
Seconds: 0	
Deciseconds: 0.1	
Centiseconds: 0.12	
Milliseconds: 0.123	
• Microseconds: 0.123456	
Nanoseconds: 0.123456789	
Display Seconds with hours and minutes	

If the **Seconds Since Beginning of Capture** option is in use, the first packet in a capture displays a time value of **0.000000**; all other packets are timed in reference to this first packet such that the elapsed time from the beginning of the capture is displayed.

The time display menu options provide examples of their formats and are fairly self-explanatory, except perhaps **Seconds Since Previous Captured Packet** and **Seconds Since Previous Displayed Packet**. The **Seconds Since Previous Captured Packet** option provides the elapsed time between each captured packet, while the **Seconds Since Previous Displayed Packet** option displays the elapsed time from the previous packet that is visible when a display filter is applied.

The way the **Displayed Packet** option works is illustrated in the following screenshot. You can see how the **Captured Packet** timestamps continue to increment, while the **Displayed Packet** timestamps show the time since the last displayed packet.

Captured Packet	Displayed Packet
0.000000	0.000000
0.001000	0.001000
0.002000	-------------
0.003000	0.002000
0.004000	-------------
0.005000	-------------
0.006000	-------------
0.007000	0.004000

The time display precision options in the **Time Display Format** menu are also shown with examples of the display format and are self-explanatory, except for the **Automatic (File Format Precision)** setting, which requires a description.

Wireshark relies on the NIC driver and the capture devices' system clock for packet timestamps. The accuracy of these timestamps in terms of the precision and number of subsecond digits (milliseconds, microseconds, and nanoseconds) will vary, but usually a millisecond resolution is available. This precision value is saved in the capture file. The **Automatic (File Format Precision)** setting tells Wireshark to display timestamps using this precision value.

The ability to use the **Nanoseconds precision** setting depends on having an NIC driver that supports this level of precision. If you select this option and the capture file doesn't contain the higher resolution, the last three digits of each timestamp will be all zeroes.

Adding a time column

It is often helpful to have two (or more) time columns in the **Packet List** pane to provide a variety of time display types without having to change the format of a single time column back and forth. You can add a new time column using one of two methods.

The following is the first method, the preferences settings method:

1. Go to **Preferences** from the **Edit** menu, or click on the **Preferences** icon to open the **Preferences** window.
2. Select **Columns**.
3. Click on **Add** to add a new entry at the bottom of the list.
4. Click on the **Title** area of the new entry and give the column a name.
5. Ensure that the new entry is highlighted, and select the desired time display format from the drop-down **Field type** box.
6. Click and drag the new entry up the list to select its relative position in the **Packet List** pane.
7. Finally, click on **OK**.

The selectable options in the **Field type** box for time display columns include the following:

- **Absolute date, as YYYY-MM-DD, and time**: This is the actual capture date and time based on the time zone of the capture device.
- **Absolute date, as YYYY/DOY, and time**: This is another format to display the date and time based on the time zone of the capture device.

- **Relative time**: This is the time from the first packet in a capture file. This is similar to the **Seconds Since Beginning of Capture** option.

- **Relative time (conversation)**: This is the time from the first packet in the trace file for a conversation (this doesn't work).

- **Delta time**: This is the elapsed time from the previous packet to the current packet.

- **Delta time (conversation)**: This is the time from the previous packet to the current packet in a conversation (this doesn't work).

- **Delta time displayed**: This is the time from the end of one packet to the end of the next displayed packet only.

- **Custom**: The **Relative time (conversation)** and **Delta time (conversation)** options, which are also listed in the preferences settings, no longer work in the version of Wireshark currently available (v1.12) as of this writing. You can accomplish the previously offered functionality with these options by using the **Custom** option with display filter-style **Field** types instead. Select the **Custom Field** type and enter either `tcp.time_relative` or `tcp.time_delta` in the **Field name** field, leaving the **Field occurrence** field with the default entry of **0**.

An example of creating a functional **Delta time (conv)** time column using the **Custom** option and the **tcp.time_delta** display filter is shown in the following screenshot:

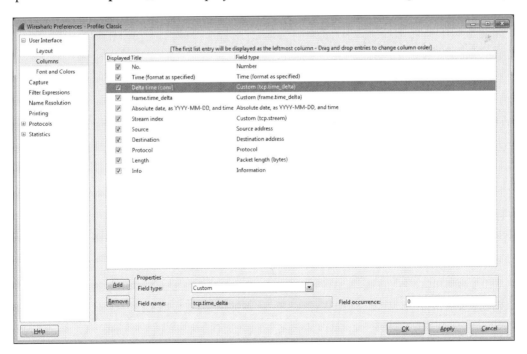

For the **tcp.time_relative** and **tcp.time_delta** fields to work properly, you must also enable **Calculate conversation timestamps** in the preferences settings using the following steps:

1. In the **Preferences** window, select **TCP** from the **Protocols** menu.

2. Enable the **Calculate conversation timestamps** option.

3. Finally, click on **OK**.

An example of enabling **Calculate conversation timestamps** is depicted in the following screenshot:

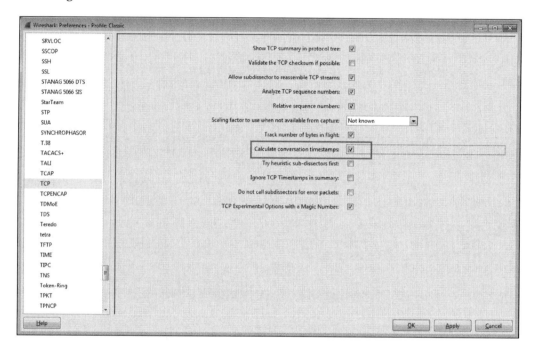

The following steps show you the second method, the right-click method of adding a column:

1. Select an appropriate packet in the **Packet List** pane.

2. In the **Packet Details** pane, expand the **Frame** header, or if applicable, expand the **Transmission Control Protocol** header.

3. Locate the desired time value field in the **Frame** or **TCP** sections (these are surrounded by brackets). If you are selecting a time value in the TCP section, you will need to expand the **[Timestamps]** section to see the values.

4. Right-click on the desired time field and select **Apply as Column** from the menu.

5. The new column will appear beside the **Info** column in the **Packet List** pane. Click and drag the new column to the desired location.

6. You can right-click on the new column header, select **Edit Column Details**, and give the column a shorter name if desired.

As previously discussed in the preferences settings method, you must enable **Calculate conversation timestamps** in the **TCP** protocol option of the preferences settings to view and use the time values in the **TCP** section.

Conversation versus displayed packet time options

The difference between time displays for a conversation versus a displayed packet time option is perhaps subtle but important.

As illustrated previously, if you are using one of the displayed packet time options, the time value shown for a given packet will be the elapsed time since the previous packet was displayed in the **Packet List** pane. This time value option has no useful value until you apply a display filter, after which you can easily see the elapsed time between each packet being displayed with no other mental math or adjustments necessary. This is very useful if you're sequentially filtering, clearing, and viewing more than one conversation using, for example, a **tcp.stream==xx** display filter setting.

If you are not using a display filter, however, there may be packets from multiple conversations displayed in the **Packet List** pane. If you are using one of the conversations time displays, the time value shown for a given packet will be the elapsed time since the previous packet for that conversation, regardless of other packets that may be interspersed and visible between the packet you're looking at and the previous packet in that conversation. This allows a quick perusal of conversation packet times without having to apply a display filter.

Choosing the best Wireshark time display option

With so many time display options available, it may be difficult to know when and where to use a given option. Choosing the optimal time display in a Wireshark time column depends greatly upon the objectives of the analysis:

- If you need to know the specific date and time of day when an event occurred in a capture, as might be the case if you're trying to find and correlate packets with user-reported events or log entries, you should use one of the **Absolute time** formats.

- If you're looking for an event that occurred some known period of time after a capture started, use one of the **Relative time** formats.

- On the other hand, if you just need to measure the time between certain packets, such as when measuring the time between a request and a response, one of the **Delta time** formats will be the most helpful.

Using the Time Reference option

Another useful Wireshark feature is the **Time Reference** menu option, which can be used to measure time from one packet to another in the midst of a capture file. You can click on a specific packet and toggle this option on and off for that packet using either the **Set/Unset Time Reference** option from the **Edit** menu, or by right-clicking and selecting the **Set Time Reference (toggle)** option from the pop-up menu. The packet will be marked with a *REF* designator in the first time column, and any relative timestamps following the **Time Reference** packet will be displayed relative to that packet.

The **Time Reference** setting is temporary; it isn't saved to a capture file and will disappear if you reload the file.

Colorization and coloring rules

Colorization of packets displayed in the **Packet List** pane can be an effective tool to identify and highlight packets of interest, especially the packets that contain or indicate some kind of error condition.

Wireshark has predefined coloring rules that are enabled by default and which can result in a kaleidoscope of colored packets in the **Packet List** pane. You can enable or disable the coloring rules by selecting **Colorize Packet List** from the **View** menu or by clicking on the **Colorize Packet List** icon in the icon bar if this becomes overwhelming.

You can also view, enable/disable, add, delete, reorder, and edit the coloring rules by selecting **Coloring Rules** from the **View** menu or by clicking on the **Edit Coloring Rules** icon in the icon bar. There is a **Clear** button that removes all the changes you may have made to the rules and restores them to default settings if needed.

A **Coloring Rules** window is depicted in the following screenshot:

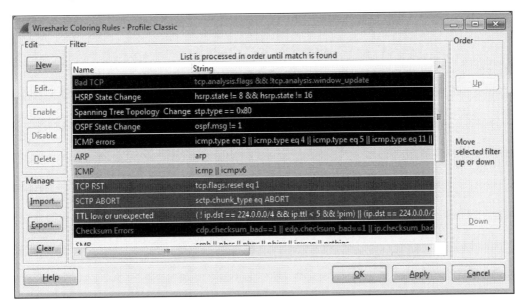

Coloring rules employ display filter formats with specific values to identify packets that should be colored. The rules are compared to packets starting with the top rule and working down through the list. Only the first rule that matches a packet's condition is applied, so the ordering of the rules dictates which rule gets applied if more than one rule matches a packet. If you create or modify a rule, you have to check the ordering to make sure you get the desired behavior.

Clicking on a rule and then clicking on **Edit** allows you to modify the foreground and background colors for that rule, as well as change the filter string if desired.

You can also export/import coloring rules if you want to share them with others. Coloring rules are stored in a file called `colorfilters` in one of your personal configuration directories depending on the profile in use.

Packet colorization

You can also temporarily color a series of packets in a conversation by selecting one of the conversation packets, selecting **Colorize Conversation** from the **View** menu, and selecting a color from the adjoining menu, or by right-clicking on a packet, selecting **Colorize Conversation** from the menu, selecting one of the protocol-specific options, and then selecting the desired color. This colorization will disappear when the capture file is reloaded, or you can select **Reset Coloring 1-10** from the **View** menu.

Wireshark preferences

In the *Adding a time column* section, we opened the **Preferences** window using **Preferences** in the **Edit** menu or by clicking on the **Preferences** icon in the icon bar to configure the time display column options. There are quite a number of **Preferences** options that you should be aware of and may want to adjust to customize your Wireshark environment:

- **Layout**: This is used to select the ordering of the **Packet List**, **Packet Details**, and **Packet Bytes** panes.

- **Columns**: This is used to add, remove, and move columns in the **Packet List** pane.

- **Capture**: This is used to set the default capture options.

- **Filter Expressions**: This is used to add, remove, or move the **Filter Expression** buttons.

- **Name Resolution**: This is used to set the MAC, transport, and network (IP) resolution options.

- **Protocols**: There are options that can be set for all of the protocols that Wireshark supports; some of the most important and useful of these options include:

  - **HTTP**: This is used to add any additional TCP ports that should be recognized as HTTP traffic in your environment.

  - **IEEE 802.11**: This is used to add/edit the **Wireless Decryption** keys if needed to decode an encrypted wireless session.

  - **IPv4**: You may want to disable **Validate IPv4 checksum if possible** to avoid inadvertent error messages caused by an **NIC** option called checksum offloading, wherein checksums are checked after the packet is sent to Wireshark.

- ○ **RTP**: Enable **Allow subdissector to reassemble RTP streams** to support decoding audio from VoIP captures.

- ○ **SMB**: Enable **Reassemble SMB Transaction payload** to support exporting file objects from an SMB stream in a packet capture.

- ○ **SSL**: Wireshark can decrypt the SSL/TLS traffic if you have the private key file. To add a key to Wireshark, go to the **Preferences** window and click on the **RSA keys list Edit** button. Then, in the **SSL Decrypt** window, click on **New** and complete the **SSL Decrypt: New** fields (**IP address** of the SSL server; **Port**, which is usually 443 for HTTP; **Protocol**, such as HTTP; and **Key File**, which is used to select the path to an RSA private key (if the key file is a PKCS#12 keystore (usually has a `.pfx` or `.p12` extension), the **Password** field must be completed)), and finally, click on **OK** to close each subsequent window.

- ○ **TCP**: This provides you with multiple options, as follows:

  - ○ **Validate TCP checksum if possible**: Disable this to avoid inadvertent error messages caused by checksum offloading.

  - ○ **Allow subdissector to reassemble TCP streams**: Enable this to support exporting file objects from a TCP stream.

  - ○ **Relative sequence numbers**: Enable this to make it easier to read and track TCP sequence numbers in a capture file.

  - ○ **Track number of bytes in flight**: This is a value calculated and displayed in the TCP protocol header in the **Packet Details** pane, which is useful for performance analysis.

  - ○ **Calculate conversation timestamps**: This is the setting discussed earlier that is needed to support the **tcp.time_ relative** and **tcp.time_delta** time displays.

There are numerous other preferences settings that may be pertinent to your personal preference or analysis environment; you will have to investigate most or all of these options. If you are unsure of a particular setting, you can get more information by clicking on the **Help** button at the bottom of the **Preferences** window.

The preferences settings are stored in a file called `preferences` in one of your **Personal configuration** directories, depending on the profile in use.

Wireshark profiles

As we have covered the numerous Wireshark configuration options that are saved in specific files, such as cfilters for **Capture Filters**, dfilters for **Display Filters**, colorfilters for **Coloring Rules**, and preferences for preferences settings, it was mentioned that these files were saved in one of your **Personal configuration** directories, but I have left a full explanation of profiles and these configuration directories until now so that you would better understand what makes up a profile and why they are useful.

A profile is a collection of Wireshark configuration files customized for your specific needs and tastes in capture and display filters, coloring rules, columns and layouts, and so on for the particular environment you are working in. You can create one or more profiles and quickly reconfigure Wireshark to work best in differing environments by selecting the appropriate profile.

When you first install Wireshark, it operates with a default set of configuration files that are located in the **Global configuration** directory, which is usually the same as the **System** directory where the Wireshark program files reside. When you change any of the default settings, the changes are saved in new configuration files that are stored in a **Personal configuration** directory, the location of which varies depending upon your installation. You can determine and quickly open the **Personal configuration** directory for your installation from Wireshark by clicking on the **About Wireshark** option in the **Help** menu and clicking on the **Folders** tab. Within this tab is a list of all the directories that Wireshark uses, as shown in the following screenshot:

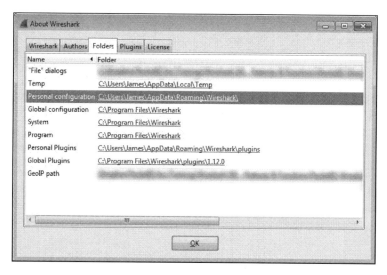

You can double-click on a Wireshark directory link to open a window to that directory.

Double-clicking on the **Personal configuration** link in the **Folders** tab opens the directory where (under a `profiles` subdirectory) your custom profile files are stored. Each profile is stored in a separate subdirectory that reflects the name you give a profile, as shown in the following screenshot:

Each custom `profile` directory contains all the Wireshark configuration files that determine how that profile controls Wireshark's features. You can copy and share these custom profile directories with other Wireshark users; copying the `profile` directory into their **Personal configuration** directory makes that profile available for selection.

Creating a Wireshark profile

To create a new Wireshark profile, follow these steps:

1. Right-click on the **Profile** section (on the right-hand side pane) of **Status Bar** at the bottom of the Wireshark user interface and click on **New**, or navigate to **Edit | Configuration Profiles | New** in the menu bar.

2. In the **Create New Profile** window that appears, you can give the profile a name. You can also choose to create the profile starting with the settings from an existing profile by making a selection from the **Create from** drop-down list or start from scratch. The **Create New Profile** window is shown in the following screenshot:

3. Clicking on **OK** will save the new profile in its own directory by the same name in your `Profiles` directory in the **Personal configuration** menu.

Selecting a Wireshark profile

You can select one of your custom profiles by selecting **Configuration Profiles** from the **Edit** menu, clicking on one of the listed profiles, and clicking on **OK**. A quicker method is just clicking on the **Profile** section of **Status Bar** and selecting a profile from the pop-up menu, as shown in the following screenshot:

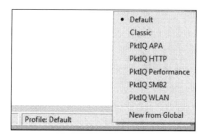

Summary

The topics covered in this chapter included working with Wireshark's time displays, colorization and coloring rules, selecting the appropriate Wireshark preferences for a given analysis environment, and saving all of these settings in profiles that can be selected as required.

In the next chapter, we'll cover a selection of network layer, transport layer, and application layer protocols in common use in modern networks, which will help you to prepare for more advanced packet analysis activities in the later chapters.

5
Network Protocols

Effective packet analysis requires familiarity with the primary protocols in use in modern networks. In this chapter, we will review the most common protocols in their respective layers:

- Network layer protocols
- Transport layer protocols
- Application layer protocols

We'll cover the significant purpose and relevant fields to support network connectivity and/or application functionality in each protocol, as well a sampling of Wireshark capture and display filters for each protocol.

The OSI and DARPA reference models

We reviewed the purpose of the OSI and DARPA reference models in *Chapter 2, Networking for Packet Analysts*. The visual depiction of their layers is repeated in the following diagram as a reference and summary of some of the primary protocols and where they fit into their respective layers:

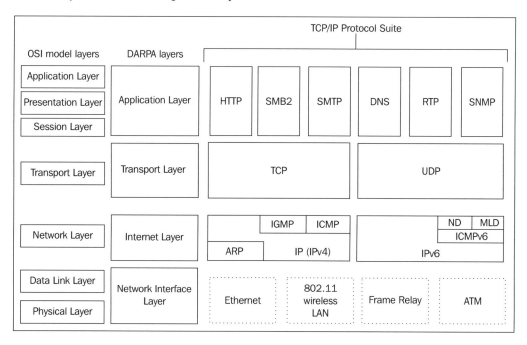

Network layer protocols

Network layer protocols, also known as Internet layer protocols in the DARPA reference model, provide basic network connectivity and internetwork communications services. In this layer, you will predominantly find the IP protocol being used to get packets transported across the network, along with ARP, IGMP, and ICMP.

We covered the IP and ARP protocol packet header structures and fields in *Chapter 2, Networking for Packet Analysts*, so this information won't be repeated. However, basic Wireshark capture and display filters are provided here and also for the remaining protocols in the following sections:

Wireshark IPv4 filters

Capture filter(s): `ip`

Display filter(s): `ip ip.addr==192.168.1.1 ip.src== ip.dst== ip.id > 2000`

Wireshark ARP filters

Capture filter(s): `arp`

Display filter(s): `arp      arp.opcode==1 arp.src.hw_`
`mac==00:1c:25:99:db:85`

Internet Group Management Protocol

The **Internet Group Management Protocol (IGMP)** is used by hosts to notify adjacent routers of established multicast (one-to-any) group memberships. In other words, IGMP enables a computer that provides content (video feeds), for example, to provide such content to a distributed group of users using one set of the multicast address ranges (in the `224.0.0.0` to `239.255.255.255` class D multicast range). This multicast capability depends on routers that are capable and configured to support this service; clients must join the multicast group. When a host wants to start a multicast, it sends an **IGMP Membership Report** message to the `224.0.0.2` (all multicast routers) address that specifies the multicast IP address for this particular group. Clients who wish to join or leave this group (so they can receive the multicast content) send an IGMP join or leave message to the router. The following table shows the various ranges for addresses:

Starting address range	Ending address range	Description
`224.0.0.0`	`224.0.0.255`	These are reserved for special well-known multicast addresses
`224.0.1.0`	`238.255.255.255`	These are globally-scoped (Internet-wide) multicast addresses
`239.0.0.0`	`239.255.255.255`	These are locally-scoped and administered multicast addresses

The following screenshot shows the significant fields in the IGMP protocol header:

```
Source            Destination        Protocol  Length   Info
192.168.0.100     224.0.0.22         IGMPv3    54       Membership Report / Join group 224.0.1.60
192.168.0.100     224.0.0.22         IGMPv3    54       Membership Report / Join group 224.0.0.252
192.168.0.100     224.0.0.22         IGMPv3    54       Membership Report / Join group 239.255.255.250
192.168.0.100     224.0.0.22         IGMPv3    54       Membership Report / Leave group 239.255.255.250

⊞ Frame 4: 54 bytes on wire (432 bits), 54 bytes captured (432 bits) on interface 0
⊟ Ethernet II, Src: 00:18:de:d0:27:d7 (00:18:de:d0:27:d7), Dst: IPv4mcast_16 (01:00:5e:00:00:16)
   ⊞ Destination: IPv4mcast_16 (01:00:5e:00:00:16)
   ⊞ Source: 00:18:de:d0:27:d7 (00:18:de:d0:27:d7)
     Type: IP (0x0800)
⊟ Internet Protocol Version 4, Src: 192.168.0.100 (192.168.0.100), Dst: 224.0.0.22 (224.0.0.22)
     Version: 4
     Header Length: 24 bytes
   ⊞ Differentiated Services Field: 0x00 (DSCP 0x00: Default; ECN: 0x00: Not-ECT (Not ECN-Capable Transport))
     Total Length: 40
     Identification: 0x000f (15)
   ⊞ Flags: 0x00
     Fragment offset: 0
     Time to live: 1
     Protocol: IGMP (2)
   ⊞ Header checksum: 0x839e [validation disabled]
     Source: 192.168.0.100 (192.168.0.100)
     Destination: 224.0.0.22 (224.0.0.22)
     [Source GeoIP: Unknown]
     [Destination GeoIP: Unknown]
   ⊞ Options: (4 bytes), Router Alert
⊟ Internet Group Management Protocol
     [IGMP Version: 3]
     Type: Membership Report (0x22)
     Header checksum: 0xeb03 [correct]
     Num Group Records: 1
   ⊟ Group Record : 239.255.255.250  Change To Include Mode
       Record Type: Change To Include Mode (3)
       Aux Data Len: 0
       Num Src: 0
       Multicast Address: 239.255.255.250 (239.255.255.250)
```

The preceding significant fields in the IGMP protocol header include:

- **Type**: This is a type of IGMP message. Type 22 is IGMPv3 **Membership Report**.

- **Record Type**: There are different types of **Group Records**. The value of **Record Type 3** is **Change To Include Mode**, which indicates that content from the source device is to be forwarded to the in-group hosts by the multicast router.

- **Multicast Address**: This is the multicast IP address for a specific group.

You should also note the following interesting fields in the previous protocol layers:

- The Ethernet frame destination MAC address is one of a range of multicast MAC addresses (01:00:5e:00:00:00 - 01:00:5e:7f:ff:ff)

- The **Protocol** field in the IP header specifies IGMP **2**

- The IP layer destination IP Address is 224.0.0.22, which is a reserved IGMPv3 multicast IP address

The IGMP protocol has multiple versions and is rather complex. Refer to the protocol references provided at the beginning of this chapter for more information.

Wireshark IGMP filters

Capture filter(s): `igmp`

Display filter(s): `igmp` `igmp.type==0x22 igmp.record_type==4 igmp.`
`maddr==244.0.1.60`

Internet Control Message Protocol

The **Internet Control Message Protocol (ICMP)** is used by network devices such
as routers to send error messages indicating that a requested service is not available,
or a host or network router could not be reached. ICMP is a control protocol. This
means that although it is transported as IP datagrams, it does not carry the application
data—instead, it carries the information about the status of the network itself.

ICMP pings

One of the most well-known uses of ICMP is to ping, wherein a device sends an
ICMP echo request (**Type 8**, **Code 0**) packet to a distant host (via that host's IP
address), which will (if the ICMP service isn't disabled or blocked by an intermediate
firewall) respond with an ICMP echo reply (**Type 0**, **Code 0**) packet. Pings are
used to determine whether the target host is available and can be reached over the
network. By measuring the time that expires between ping requests and replies, we
know the **round trip time** (**RTT**) delay time over the network path.

ICMP traceroutes

A variation of ping functionality is used to perform a traceroute (also known as
traceroute), which is a list of the IP addresses of the router interfaces that packets
traverse to get from a sending device to a target host or device. The traceroutes are
used to determine or confirm the network path taken from a sending device to a
target host or device.

A traceroute is accomplished by sending the ICMP echo request packets to a distant
host just as in a normal ping, but with modifications to the **Time-to-Live** (**TTL**)
field in the IP header of each packet. The traceroute function takes advantage of
the fact that each router in a network path decrements the TTL value in a packet by
1, so as the packet traverses, the routers in a path and the TTL value will decrease
accordingly along the way. If a router receives a packet with a TTL value of 1, it will
send an ICMP TTL exceeded in transit (**Type 11**, **Code 0**) error message back to the
sender (along with a copy of the request packet it received) and otherwise discard
(not forward) the packet.

The traceroute works by sequentially setting the TTL in multiple ICMP request packets to 1, then to 2, then 3, and so on, which results in each router in the network path sending TTL exceeded error messages back to the sender. Since these returned messages are sent by the in-path router using the IP address of the interface where the ICMP packet was received, the traceroute utility can build and display a progressive list of router interface IP addresses in the path and the RTT delay to each router.

ICMP control message types

A sampling of the most commonly seen types of ICMP control messages, including their type and code (subtype) numbers, are provided in the following table:

Type	Code	Description
0	0	This indicates echo reply (ping)
3	0	This indicates destination network unreachable
3	1	This indicates destination host unreachable
3	4	This indicates fragmentation required and do not fragment bit set
3	6	This indicates destination network unknown
3	7	This indicates destination host unknown
5	0	This indicates redirect datagram for the network
5	1	This indicates redirect datagram for the host
8	0	This indicates echo request (ping)
11	0	This indicates TTL expired in transit (seen in traceroutes)

The Wireshark packet details fields for the ICMP packet illustrated in the following screenshot depict a **Time-to-live exceeded** message as seen in a typical traceroute capture:

```
⊞ Frame 13: 70 bytes on wire (560 bits), 70 bytes captured (560 bits)
⊞ Ethernet II, Src: c8:d7:19:21:b7:ec (c8:d7:19:21:b7:ec), Dst: 00:1c:25:99:db:85 (00:1c:
⊞ Internet Protocol Version 4, Src: 10.192.128.1 (10.192.128.1), Dst: 192.168.1.115 (192.
⊟ Internet Control Message Protocol
    Type: 11 (Time-to-live exceeded)
    Code: 0 (Time to live exceeded in transit)
    Checksum: 0x2161 [correct]
  ⊟ Internet Protocol Version 4, Src: 192.168.1.115 (192.168.1.115), Dst: 205.251.242.54
      Version: 4
      Header Length: 20 bytes
    ⊞ Differentiated Services Field: 0x00 (DSCP 0x00: Default; ECN: 0x00: Not-ECT (Not EC
      Total Length: 56
      Identification: 0x637d (25469)
    ⊞ Flags: 0x02 (Don't Fragment)
      Fragment offset: 0
    ⊞ Time to live: 1
      Protocol: ICMP (1)
    ⊞ Header checksum: 0x93fa [validation disabled]
      Source: 192.168.1.115 (192.168.1.115)
      Destination: 205.251.242.54 (205.251.242.54)
      [Source GeoIP: Unknown]
      [Destination GeoIP: Unknown]
  ⊟ Internet Control Message Protocol
      Type: 8 (Echo (ping) request)
      Code: 0
      Checksum: 0xc739
      Identifier (BE): 1 (0x0001)
      Identifier (LE): 256 (0x0100)
      Sequence number (BE): 1124 (0x0464)
      Sequence number (LE): 25604 (0x6404)
```

The following points are significant to analyze this packet:

- The source IP address seen in the IPv4 header summary is **10.192.128.1**, which is the IP address of the router interface sending the ICMP message to the originator, **192.168.1.115**

- The ICMP packet is **Type 11**, **Code 0** (TTL exceeded in transit)

The second set of IPv4 and ICMP headers that follow the first IPv4 and ICMP headers are copies of the original packet transmitted by the sender. This copy is returned to allow determination of the packet that caused the ICMP message. The significant points in the packet details of this ICMP message copy include:

- The target destination IP address, where the echo request packet was intended to be sent (and would have been if the TTL value hadn't been altered) is 205.251.242.51.

- The TTL value was **1** when this packet reached the 10.192.128.1 router interface. This packet cannot be forwarded, resulting in the TTL exceeded message being sent back to the sender.

- The original ICMP packet was a **Type 8**, **Code 0** echo request message.

- The **Header Data** section of the ICMP packet for the echo requests and replies will include a 16-bit identifier and 16-bit sequence number, which are used to match echo replies to their requests.

ICMP redirects

Another common use of ICMP is to redirect a client to use a different default gateway (router) to reach a host or network than the gateway it originally tried to use. In the ICMP **Redirect** packet depicted in the following screenshot, a number of packet fields should be noted:

- The source IP address of the ICMP redirect packet is 192.168.1.1, which was the client's default gateway; this is the router sending the redirect packet back to the client

- The ICMP **Type** is **5** (**Redirect**) and **Code** is **1** (**Redirect for host**)

- The gateway IP address that the router 192.168.1.1 is telling the client to use to reach the desired target host is 192.168.1.2

- The IP address of the target host was 10.1.1.125

The following screenshot shows the ICMP **Redirect** packets:

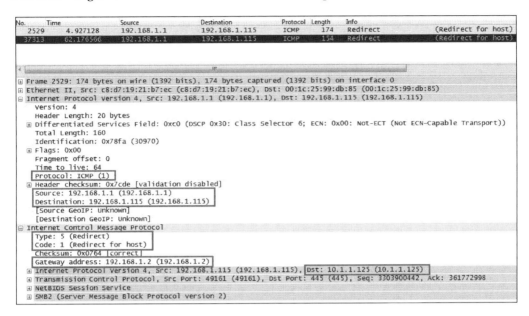

Wireshark ICMP filters

Capture filters(s): `icmp`

Display filter(s): `icmp`   `icmp.type==8 || icmp.type==0 (pings)`
`icmp.type==5`
`&& icmp.code==1 (host redirects)`

Internet Protocol Version 6

The **Internet Protocol Version 6 (IPv6)** is the latest version of Internet protocol, and although it is in its earliest stages of adoption, it is intended to eventually replace IPv4—mostly to alleviate the shortage of IP addresses that can be assigned to network devices. IPv4, with its 32-bit address space, provides approximately 4.3 billion addresses, nearly all of which have been assigned to companies and private interests worldwide.

IPv6 utilizes a 128-bit address space, which allows 2^{128} or approximately 3.4×10^{38} addresses; that number is 340,282,366,920,463,463,374,607,431,768,211,456 unique addresses.

IPv6 addressing

The 128 bits of an IPv6 address are represented in eight groups of 16 bits each, written as four hexadecimal digits separated by colons (:). An example of an IPv6 address is `2001:0db8:0000:0000:0000:ff00:0042:8329`.

For convenience, an IPv6 address may be abbreviated to shorter notations by application of the following rules, wherever possible:

- One or more leading zeroes from any groups of hexadecimal digits are removed; this is usually done to either all or none of the leading zeroes. For example, the hexadecimal group 0042 can be converted to just 42.

- Consecutive sections of zeroes are replaced with a double colon (::). The double colon may only be used once in an address, as multiple use would render the address indeterminate. A double colon must not be used to denote a single section of omitted zeroes.

An example of applying these rules to IPv6 addresses is as follows:

- **Initial address**: `2001:0db8:0000:0000:0000:ff00:0042:8329`
- **After removing all leading zeroes**: `2001:db8:0:0:0:ff00:42:8329`
- **After omitting consecutive sections of zeroes**: `2001:db8::ff00:42:8329`

The 128 bits of an IPv6 address are logically divided into a network prefix and a host identifier. The **Class Inter-Domain Routing (CIDR)** notation is used to represent IPv6 network prefixes, for example, `2001:DB8:0:CD30::/64` represents network `2001:DB8:0000:CD30::`.

IPv6 address types

There are three basic types of IPv6 addresses:

- **Unicast**: These packets from one-to-one device use a single interface address. Unicast addresses can be of one of the following three types:
    - **Global Unicast**: This is routable to and over the Internet. Global Unicast addresses generally start with 2xxx (such as `2000::/3`).

- ◦ **Link-local**: This is automatically assigned to an interface and used on the local network link; this is not routable to the Internet, much like a MAC address. Link-local Unicast addresses start with FE80 (FE80::/10). They are automatically assigned to an interface when it is initialized using an algorithm that uses a rearranged version of the NIC's 48-bit MAC address in the IPv6 address and are used to communicate on the local link. These addresses are not routable. IPv6 uses link-local addresses for neighbor discovery functions.

- ◦ **Unique local**: This is not routable to the Internet, but it is routable within an enterprise (similar to IPv4 private addresses). Unique local Unicast addresses start with FC00 (FC00::/7). This block of addresses is reserved for use in private IPv6 networks.

- **Multicast**: These are packets from one-to-many devices. Multicast addresses start with FFxx. An example of a multicast address is FF01:0:0:0:0:0:0:101, which can be shortened to FF01::101. There is no broadcast address in IPv6; multicasts are used as a replacement. Some well-known multicast addresses are shown in the following table:

Address	Description	Scope
ff01:0:0:0:0:0:0:1	All nodes address	Interface-local (spans only a single interface on a node useful only for loopback transmission of multicast packets)
ff02:0:0:0:0:0:0:1	All nodes address	Link-local (all nodes on the local network segment)
ff01:0:0:0:0:0:0:2	All routers address	Interface-local
ff02:0:0:0:0:0:0:2	All routers address	Link-local
ff05:0:0:0:0:0:0:2	All routers address	Site-local (spans a single site)
ff02:0:0:0:0:0:1:2	DHCPv6 servers/agents	Link-local
ff05:0:0:0:0:0:1:3	DHCPv6 servers/agents	Site-local

- **Anycast**: These packets are from one to the nearest of a group of interfaces. There is no special addresses scheme for Anycast addresses; they are similar to Unicast addresses. An Anycast address is created automatically when a Unicast address is assigned to more than one interface. Anycast addresses can be used to set up a group of devices so that any one of the group devices can respond to a request sent to a single IPv6 address.

Further discussion of IPv6 addressing would cover quite a number of additional features, which are beyond the scope of this book. The reader is encouraged to research IPv6 addressing further online and/or by reading Request For Comments (RFC) 4291 (IP Version 6 Addressing Architecture).

IPv6 header fields

An example of an IPv6 protocol header is illustrated in the following screenshot:

```
⊟ Internet Protocol Version 6, Src: 2607:f0d0:2001:e:1::120 (2607:f0d0:2001:
  ⊞ 0110 .... = Version: 6
  ⊞ .... 0000 0000 .... .... .... .... .... = Traffic class: 0x00000000
    .... .... .... 0000 0000 0000 0000 0000 = Flowlabel: 0x00000000
    Payload length: 428
    Next header: TCP (6)
    Hop limit: 50
    Source: 2607:f0d0:2001:e:1::120 (2607:f0d0:2001:e:1::120)
    Destination: 2002:1806:addc::1806:addc (2002:1806:addc::1806:addc)
    [Source GeoIP: Unknown]
    [Destination GeoIP: Unknown]
⊟ Transmission Control Protocol, Src Port: 80 (80), Dst Port: 52004 (52004),
```

The IPv6 header fields are similar to many IPv4 headers and the fields include:

- **Version**: This is the IP version number, 6 for IPv6.

- **Traffic class**: This is similar to the IPv4 **DiffServ** field; it is used to identify different classes or priorities of IPv6 packets.

- **Flow label**: These are used to identify sequences of packets that are labeled as a set. An IPv6 flow is defined by the 20-bit **Flow Label** field and the source and destination IPv6 address fields.

- **Payload length**: This is the length of the IPv6 payload, not including any packet padding.

- **Next header**: This field indicates what's coming next in the packet. This is equivalent to the IPv4 **Protocol** field. In the preceding example, the next layer is a normal **TCP (6)** header.

- **Hop limit**: This field is roughly equivalent to the **Time To Live** field in IPv4; it is decremented by one by each device that forwards the IPv6 packet. When the value reaches one, the packet cannot be forwarded.

- **Source and Destination addresses**: These are the 128-bit IPv6 source and destination addresses.

IPv6 supports extension headers that provide additional information fields and that also extend the length of the IPv6 header. There is specific **Next Header** code that indicates the presence of this added functionality.

IPv6 transition methods

As part of the transition to IPv6, the current TCP/IP devices support dual stacks (IPv4 and IPv6 simultaneously) and the ability to encapsulate and tunnel IPv6 packets inside IPv4 packets so that they can be routed by IPv4 networks. The three of the most popular encapsulation methods are:

- **6to4 tunneling**: In this tunneling method, an IPv6 header follows an IPv4 header; the **Protocol** field of the IPv4 header will contain 41 (IPv6), and the source IPv6 address in the IPv6 header will start with 2002.

- **Teredo**: In this tunneling method, an IPv6 header is encapsulated inside a UDP packet. This method was developed to accommodate NAT devices that do not handle protocol 41. Teredo tunneling can be identified in the UDP packet header by a destination port of 3544.

- **ISATAP**: This tunneling method uses a locally assigned IPv4 address to create a 64-bit interface identifier. For example, in ISATAP, the IPv4 address 24.6.173.220 becomes ::0:5EFE:1806:addc. ISATAP encapsulates IPv6 headers within IPv4 as in 6to4 tunneling.

Wireshark IPv6 filters

Capture filter(s): ip6   host fe80::1   ip proto 41 (capture IPv6-over-IPv4 tunneled traffic)

Display filter(s): ipv6   ipv6.addr == fe80::f61f:c2ff:fe58:7dcb ipv6.addr == ff02::1

Internet Control Message Protocol Version 6

Internet Control Message Protocol Version 6 (ICMPv6) is an integral part of IPv6, and the base protocol must be fully implemented by every IPv6 node. ICMPv6 provides services for an IPv6 environment that are provided by other distinct protocols in an IPv4 environment, such as Neighbor Solicitation to replace ARP.

The following table contains some of the common ICMPv6 packet types:

ICMPv6 packet type	ICMPv6 type	Purpose
Echo request	128	Ping request
Echo response	129	Ping response
Multicast listener query	130	Sent by multicast router to poll a network segment for group members

ICMPv6 packet type	ICMPv6 type	Purpose
Multicast listener report	131	Sent by a host when it joins a multicast group, or in response to a multicast listener query sent by a router
Multicast listener done	132	Sent by a host when it leaves a multicast group and might be the last member of that group on the network segment
Router solicitation	133	Discover the local router(s)
Router advertisement	134	Respond to Router Solicitation messages, as well as sending this packet after initialization and periodically afterwards
Neighbor solicitation	135	Used first for Duplicate Address Detection (using a source address of : :) and then to obtain the MAC address of the local router; this function replaces ARP
Neighbor advertisement	136	Response to Neighbor Solicitation messages
Redirect message	137	Redirect a device to the proper router to send packets to a specific network or host

An example of a Neighbor Solicitation ICMPv6 packet is shown in the following screenshot:

```
⊞ Frame 1: 78 bytes on wire (624 bits), 78 bytes captured (624 bits) on interface 0
⊞ Ethernet II, Src: 00:18:de:d0:27:d7 (00:18:de:d0:27:d7), Dst: IPv6mcast_ff:c8:e5:c8 (
⊟ Internet Protocol Version 6, Src: :: (::), Dst: ff02::1:ffc8:e5c8 (ff02::1:ffc8:e5c8)
   ⊞ 0110 .... = Version: 6
   ⊞ .... 0000 0000 .... .... .... .... .... = Traffic class: 0x00000000
     .... .... .... 0000 0000 0000 0000 0000 = Flowlabel: 0x00000000
     Payload length: 24
     Next header: ICMPv6 (58)
     Hop limit: 255
     Source: :: (::)
     Destination: ff02::1:ffc8:e5c8 (ff02::1:ffc8:e5c8)
     [Source GeoIP: Unknown]
     [Destination GeoIP: Unknown]
⊟ Internet Control Message Protocol v6
     Type: Neighbor Solicitation (135)
     Code: 0
     Checksum: 0x8de8 [correct]
     Reserved: 00000000
     Target Address: fe80::85ed:bc2e:dfc8:e5c8 (fe80::85ed:bc2e:dfc8:e5c8)
```

The significant fields in this packet include:

- **Next Header**: This field contains **58**, which indicates that the next protocol header is to be ICMPv6.

- **IPv6 Source Address**: The presence of an unspecified address (::) indicates this is a **Duplicate Address Detection** packet.

- **IPv6 Destination Address**: This is basically a multicast address.

- **ICMPv6 Type**: This is a Neighbor Solicitation message using Type **135**.

- **ICMPv6 Code**: This is the subtype for Neighbor Solicitation messages; this will be **0**.

- **ICMPv6 Target Address**: This is the address the host wants to use. If another node on the network is already using this address, they will respond accordingly.

Multicast Listener Discovery

Multicast Listener Discovery (**MLD**) is another component of the IPv6 suite used by IPv6 routers to discover multicast listeners on a directly attached link. MLD is part of the ICMPv6 protocol and it replaces IGMP on IPv4 networks.

Wireshark ICMPv6 filters

Capture filter(s): `icmp6`

Display filter(s): `icmpv6`
(Neighbor Solicitation)

`icmpv6.type==1135 && icmpv6.code==0`

Transport layer protocols

The transport layer protocols include TCP and UDP used to transport application protocols.

User Datagram Protocol

The **User Datagram Protocol** (**UDP**) is considered an unreliable transport. In this, there's no guarantee of packet delivery or ordering, but it has a lower overhead and is used by time-sensitive applications such as voice and video traffic.

The following screenshot shows the fields contained in an UDP header:

```
⊞ Frame 18: 214 bytes on wire (1712 bits), 214 bytes captured (1712 bits)
⊞ Ethernet II, Src: Polycom_82:92:20 (00:04:f2:82:92:20), Dst: Cisco_55:14:b5 (00:27:0d:55:14:b5)
⊞ Internet Protocol Version 4, Src: 10.1.1.100 (10.1.1.100), Dst: 208.73.144.71 (208.73.144.71)
⊟ User Datagram Protocol, Src Port: 2222 (2222), Dst Port: 24268 (24268)
    Source port: 2222 (2222)
    Destination port: 24268 (24268)
    Length: 180
  ⊞ Checksum: 0xb64c
⊞ Real-Time Transport Protocol
```

The UDP header is only 8-bytes long, consisting of:

- **Source and Destination port number**: This is 2 bytes each.
- **Length**: This is the length of the UDP header plus the payload. This is a 2-byte field.
- **Checksum**: This is a 2-byte field used to check for errors in the UDP header and data. If no checksum was generated by the transmitter, this will be all zeroes.

Wireshark UDP filters

Capture filter(s): udp   `udp port 2222`

Display filter(s): udp   `udp.srcport == 161 (SNMP response) udp.length > 256`

Transmission Control Protocol

The **Transmission Control Protocol (TCP)** provides a reliable delivery of data by detecting lost, duplicated, or out-of-order packets, requesting retransmission of lost data, or rearranging packets in the right order before delivering them to the application. TCP can also accept a large chunk of data from an application and handle getting the data transported to the other end reliably using multiple packets and reassembling them at the other end.

The following screenshot highlights the significant fields of a basic TCP header:

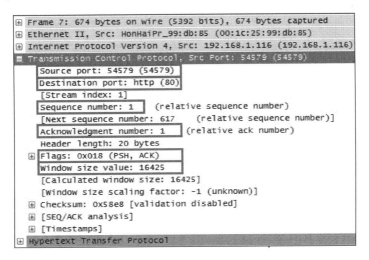

The TCP header contents and length can vary depending on options that may be in use, but in its simplest implementation it consists of:

- **Source port and Destination port**: These are well-known and registered ports are used (on servers) to access standard application services such as HTTP, FTP, SMTP, databases, and so on. Port numbers assigned to client/user sessions are usually in a higher number range and assigned sequentially.

- **Sequence number**: This is a number that represents the first octet in any given segment. Sequence numbers are initialized at the beginning of new sessions as a random number, and then incremented as data bytes are sent.

- **Acknowledgment number**: When the ACK flag bit is set, this field contains the next sequence number expected from the sender, which in turn acknowledges receipt of all the bytes received up to that point.

> The use of sequence and acknowledgment numbers is how TCP ensures reliable delivery of data by tracking the number and order of received bytes.
>
> Sequence and acknowledgment numbers are large and difficult for humans to follow. Wireshark can convert and display these as relative values that start with 0 at the beginning of a session to make it easier to inspect them and relate the values to the number of bytes transmitted and received.

- **Flags**: These bits are used to control connection setups, terminations, and flow control mechanisms.
- **Window size**: This field indicates the current size of the buffer on this host used to store received data until it can be handed off to the receiving application. This information enables the sending host to adjust data flow rates in case of network or host congestion.

TCP flags

The following table lists the flags that are most commonly used in a TCP header:

Flag field name	Description
URG (urgent)	This indicates the **Urgent Pointer** field (after the TCP header checksum) that should be examined. This flag is normally 0; the **Urgent Pointer** field is only examined if this bit is set.
ACK (acknowledgment)	This is the acknowledgment packet.
PSH (push)	This indicates whether the sending node's TCP stack should bypass any buffering and pass the data directly to the network and on to the receiving application.
RST (reset)	This is used to close the connection explicitly.
SYN (synchronize)	This is used to synchronize sequence numbers and used in a three-way TCP session initiation handshake process.
FIN (finish)	This is used when the transaction is finished. This does not mean that the connection is to be closed explicitly, but is commonly seen at the end of sessions.

TCP options

The TCP also supports a number of additional options, several of which are in common use in modern networks that you should be aware of. The snippet of a TCP header illustrated in the following screenshot depicts several of the most popular options:

```
      Window size value: 8192
      [Calculated window size: 8192]
   ⊟ Checksum: 0xcdbf [validation disabled]
         [Good Checksum: False]
         [Bad Checksum: False]
      Urgent pointer: 0
   ⊟ Options: (12 bytes), Maximum segment size
      ⊟ Maximum segment size: 1460 bytes
            Kind: Maximum Segment Size (2)
            Length: 4
            MSS Value: 1460
      ⊟ No-Operation (NOP)
         ⊟ Type: 1
               0... .... = Copy on fragmentation: No
               .00. .... = Class: Control (0)
               ...0 0001 = Number: No-Operation (NOP) (1)
      ⊟ Window scale: 2 (multiply by 4)
            Kind: Window Scale (3)
            Length: 3
            Shift count: 2
            [Multiplier: 4]
      ⊟ No-Operation (NOP)
         ⊟ Type: 1
               0... .... = Copy on fragmentation: No
               .00. .... = Class: Control (0)
               ...0 0001 = Number: No-Operation (NOP) (1)
      ⊟ No-Operation (NOP)
         ⊟ Type: 1
               0... .... = Copy on fragmentation: No
               .00. .... = Class: Control (0)
               ...0 0001 = Number: No-Operation (NOP) (1)
      ⊟ TCP SACK Permitted Option: True
            Kind: SACK Permitted (4)
            Length: 2
   ⊞ [Timestamps]
```

The TCP options highlighted in the preceding screenshot include:

- **Maximum Segment Size**: This option allows you to specify of the number of bytes that can follow the TCP header. This option exists to allow adjustment to accommodate VLAN tagging or **Multiprotocol Label Switching** (**MPLS**).

- **Window Scale**: This option overcomes the inability of the **Window Size** field in a standard TCP header to specify a window size greater than 65,535 bytes. Window scaling allows you to specify a factor to multiply the advertised window size to achieve a larger window size. Both sides of a session must be able to support this option for it to apply; this is determined during the session setup.

- **TCP SACK Permitted Option**: This option indicates that this node supports selective acknowledgments, which allows a node to acknowledge ongoing and incoming data packets while still asking for a specific missing packet. The recovery process only requires retransmission of the missing packet(s), instead of the missing packet and all the packets that followed. Both sides of a session must be able to support this option for it to apply, as determined during session setup.

Wireshark TCP filters

Capture filter(s): `tcp`   `tcp port 80`

Display filter(s): `tcp`   `tcp.port == 80 tcp.dstport == 8080 tcp.stream == 2`

Application layer protocols

The most common application layer protocols include DHCP used to obtain client IP addresses and configuration information, DNS for hostname resolution, HTTP, SMB, POP/SMTP, and FTP for the most common network services and SIP, RTP, and RTCP for VoIP and video conferencing.

Extensive coverage of all the upper layer protocols is beyond the scope of this book. A brief overview of DHCP and DNS will be provided, as these protocols universally support network operations and HTTP as an example of one of the most common application layer protocols. The reader is encouraged to research any or all of these protocols further depending on their scope of interest and need to meet the analysis tasks being addressed.

Dynamic Host Configuration Protocol

Dynamic Host Configuration Protocol (DHCP) allows a client to lease an IP address from a pool managed by a DHCP server. The client can receive other configuration options such as the default gateway, subnet mask, and one or more DNS server addresses as well. DHCP is derived from an older BOOTP protocol; Wireshark uses bootp in display filter syntax. DHCP works by the client sending a broadcast packet using UDP source port 67 to UDP destination port 68. A DHCP server will respond to the requestor's IP address and using UDP source port 68 to UDP destination port 67.

DHCP servers don't necessarily have to reside on the same local network segment as clients. A relay agent such as a router can forward DHCP requests and respond to/from a different network where a DHCP server resides.

Wireshark DHCP filters

Capture filter(s): port 67 (DHCP is between ports 67 and 68; filtering on port 67 is sufficient to get both sides of the conversations)

Display filter(s): bootp   bootp.option.value == 0 (DHCP Discover message)

Dynamic Host Configuration Protocol Version 6

Dynamic Host Configuration Protocol Version 6 (DHCPv6) is the IPv6 version of DHCP. Since IPv6 doesn't use broadcasts, DHCPv6 clients use the multicast address for All_DHCP_Relay_Agents_and_Servers (ff02::1:2) to locate DHCPv6 servers or relay agents.

Wireshark DHCPv6 filters

Capture filter(s): port 546 (DHCPv6 is between ports 546 and 547; either will work)

Display filter(s): dhcpv6   dhcpv6.msgtype == 1(DHCPv6 Solicit message)

Domain Name Service

Domain Name Service (DNS) is used to convert host names, such as www.wireshark.org to IP addresses. DNS can also be used to identify the hostname associated with an IP address (an inverse or pointer (PTR) query) and several other network information services. This is a good protocol to become familiar with as it is used extensively to locate nodes both within an enterprise and on the Internet using hostnames.

Wireshark DNS filters

Capture filter(s): port 53

Display filter(s): dns   dns.flags.response == 0(DNS query) dns.flags.response == 1(DNS response) dns.flags.rcode != 0(DNS response contains an error)

Hypertext Transfer Protocol

Hypertext Transfer Protocol (HTTP) is the application protocol used when someone browses (unsecured) websites on the Internet, along with the secure version (HTTPS). HTTP/1.1 is the current version—although HTTP/2.0 is starting to appear in some environments. Be aware that some network devices such as proxy servers and gateways may not support HTTP/2.0 yet.

An example of a HTTP packet delivering a GET request to a web server is depicted in the following screenshot:

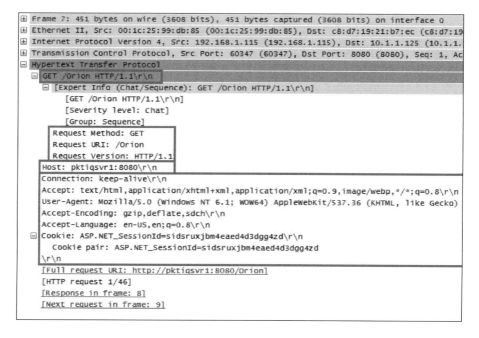

The most common features and fields of the HTTP protocol include HTTP Methods, Host, and Request Modifiers.

In the preceding screenshot, the HTTP header includes:

- **Request Method**: GET
- **Request URI**: **/Orion** (a home page on the web server)
- **Request Version**: HTTP/1.1

HTTP Methods

Some of the more common HTTP Methods are listed and described in the following table:

Method	Description
GET	This retrieves information defined by the **Uniform Resource Identifier (URI)** field
HEAD	This retrieves meta data related to the desired URI
POST	This sends data to the HTTP server/application
OPTIONS	This determines the options associated with a resource
PUT	This sends data to the HTTP server/application
DELETE	This deletes the resource defined by the URI
CONNECT	This is used to connect to a proxy device

Host

The **Host** field identifies the target host and port number of the resource being requested. In the preceding screenshot, **Host** is pktiqsvr1 on port 8080.

Request Modifiers

HTTP requests and responses use Request Modifiers to provide details for the request. In the preceding screenshot, Request Modifiers includes:

- **Connection**: This indicates the preference for a persistent connection (keep-alive).
- **Accept**: This is a list of data formats (text/html and application/xhtml plus xml) accepted.
- **User-agent**: This is a list of browser and operating system parameters (Mozilla/5.0 (Windows NT 6.1; WOW64) AppleWebKit) for the requesting device.
- **Accept-encoding**: This is a list of the acceptable HTTP compression schemes (gzip, deflate, and sdch).
- **Accept-language**: The acceptable languages (en-US and en; q=0.8) where q=0.8 is a relative quality factor that specifies the language the user would prefer on a scale of 0 to 1.
- **Cookie**: This is a session ID cookie (ASP.NET_SessionId=sidsruxjbm4eaed 4d3dgg4zd) that was previously stored on the user's browser in a cookie and is being provided to the website.

The following table lists some of the more commonly used modifiers:

Request Modifier	Description
Accept	Acceptable content types
Accept-charset	Acceptable character sets
Accept-encoding	Acceptable encodings
Accept-language	Acceptable languages
Accept-ranges	Server can accept range requests
Authorization	Authentication credentials for HTTP authentication
Cache-control	Caching directives
Connection	Type of connection preferred by the user agent
Cookie	HTTP cookie (a small piece of data sent from the website and stored in a user's browser, and/or sent back to the website the next time the user visits containing session information)
Content-length	Length of the request body in bytes
Content-type	Mime type of the body (used with POST and PUT requests)
Date	Date and time the message was sent
Expect	Defines server behavior expected by the client
If-match	Perform action if client-provided information matches
If-modified-since	Provide date/time of cached data; return **304 Not Modified** if the cached data is still current
If-range	Request for range of missing information
IF-unmodified-since	Only send if unmodified since the provided date/time
Max-forwards	Limit the number of forwards through proxies or gateways
Proxy-authorization	Authorization credential for a proxy connection
Range	Request only part of an entity
TE	Transfer encodings accepted
User-agent	A string containing browser and operating system information
Via	The proxies traversed

Wireshark HTTP filters

Capture filter(s): `tcp port http`   `tcp port https`

Display filter(s): `http`   `http.request.method == "GET" or http.request.method == "POST"` `http.response.code > 399`
(identifies client or server error packets)

Additional information

Covering all the most common upper layer protocols or covering them to any great depth is obviously more than what can be included in a book of this size. I encourage you to spend some time studying those protocols that are of interest to you for personal or job-related reasons. The return on your investment in time will be well worth the effort.

Additional information for any of the protocols discussed in this chapter as well as all those not covered can be found online.

Wireshark wiki

If you are inspecting a protocol within the Wireshark's **Packet Details** pane, you can right-click on a protocol header or field within a header and select the **Wiki Protocol Page** from the menu to go to the specific page on the Wireshark wiki that contains information on that protocol. More information can be found at `http://wiki.wireshark.org/ProtocolReference`.

You can also get a complete list of Wireshark display filters on specific protocols by selecting a protocol header or a field within a header, right-clicking, and selecting **Filter Field Reference**.

Protocols on Wikipedia

You can find general information on various protocols on Wikipedia. Start with the Internet protocol. Additional links to the entire Internet protocol suite are also provided at `http://en.wikipedia.org/wiki/Internet_Protocol`.

Requests for Comments

The **Requests for Comment (RFC)** documents contain detailed information for all the Internet protocols. These documents are maintained by the **Internet Engineering Task Force (IETF)** and are the final word on how the protocols should be implemented and function (`http://www.ietf.org/rfc.html`). If you want to search for a specific RFC by title or keyword, use the link `http://www.rfc-editor.org/search/rfc_search.php`.

Summary

The topics covered in this chapter included protocol and field coverage of the network layer protocols IPv4, ARP, IGMP, ICMP, IPv6, and ICMPv6; the transport layer protocols UDP and TCP; an overview of the application layer protocols DHCP, DHCPv6, and DNS; and a more in-depth look at HTTP.

In the next chapter, we'll put all the topics covered so far to good use by using Wireshark to troubleshoot the functionality and performance issues.

6
Troubleshooting and Performance Analysis

In this chapter, we will discuss the use of Wireshark for its primary purpose — troubleshooting network and application connectivity, functionality, and performance issues.

The topics that will be covered include:

- Troubleshooting methodology
- Troubleshooting connectivity issues
- Troubleshooting functional issues
- Performance analysis methodology
- Top five reasons for poor application performance
- Detecting and prioritizing delays
- Server processing time events
- Application turn's delay
- Network path latency
- Bandwidth congestion
- Data transport issues

These topics cover the majority of problems you'll come across in your analysis efforts.

Troubleshooting methodology

There are two fundamental reasons why you might be doing packet analysis:

- Troubleshooting a connectivity or functionality problem (a user can't connect, an application doesn't work, or doesn't work right), which we'll just call troubleshooting

- Analyzing a performance problem (the application works but is slow), which we'll call performance analysis

A third gray area is an application that basically works but is slow and occasionally times out, which could involve an underlying functional problem that causes the performance issue, or just simply be a really poor performance.

Troubleshooting a connectivity or functional issue is just a matter of comparing what normally works with what is going on, in the case you're working on.

A performance problem, on the other hand, requires determining where the majority of the time for a particular transaction to complete is being spent, measuring the delay and comparing that delay to what is normal or acceptable. The source and type of excessive delay usually points to the next area to investigate further or resolve.

In any case, you need to gather the information that allows you to determine whether this is a connectivity, functional, or performance issue and approach the problem according to its nature.

Gathering the right information

The most important thing you can do when approaching a problem is to determine what the real problem is so you can work on the right problem or the right aspect of the problem. In order to determine what the real problem is, or at least get close, you'll need to ask questions and interpret the answers. These questions could include the appropriate selections (depending on the complaint) from the following list:

- Define the problem:
    - What were you trying to do (connect to a server, log in, send/receive e-mails, general application usage, upload/download file, and specific transactions or functions)?
    - Is nothing working or is this just a problem with a specific application or multiple applications?

- What website/server/application were you trying / connecting to? Do you know the hostname, URL, and/or IP address and port used to access the application?

- What is the symptom/nature of the problem? Has this application or function/feature worked before, or is this the first time you've ever tried to use it?

- Did you receive any error messages or other indications of a problem?

- Is the issue consistent or intermittent? Depends? On what?

- How long has this been happening?

- Was there some recent change that did or could have had an impact?

- What has been identified or suspected so far? What has been done to address this? Has it helped or changed anything?

- Are there any other pertinent factors, symptoms, or recent changes to the user environment that should be considered?

- Determine the scope of the issue:

  - Is this problem occurring for a single user or a group of users?

  - Is this problem occurring within a specific office, region, or across the whole company?

  - Is this problem affecting different types of users differently?

- Collect system, application, and path information. For a more in-depth analysis (beyond single user or small group issues), the applicable questions from the following list might also need to be gathered and analyzed, as appropriate to the complaint (some of this information may have to be obtained from network or application support groups):

  - What is the browser type and version on the client (for web apps)? Is this different from clients that are working properly?

  - What is the operating system type and version of the client(s) and server?

  - What is the proper (vendor) application name and version? Are there any known issues with the application that match these symptoms (check the vendor's bug reports).

  - What is the database type and server environment behind the application server?

       ◦   Are there other backend-supporting data sources such as an online data service or Documentum and SharePoint servers involved?

       ◦   What is the network path between the client and server? Are there firewalls, proxy servers, load balancers, and/or WAN accelerators in the path? Are they configured and working properly?

       ◦   Can you confirm the expected network path (and any WAN links involved) with a traceroute and verify the bandwidth availability?

       ◦   Can you measure the **round trip time (RTT)** path latency from the user to the application server with pings or TCP handshake completion times?

Establishing the general nature of the problem

At this point, you should be able to identify the general nature of the problem between one of the following three basic types:

- Determine whether this is a connectivity problem

  ◦   User(s) cannot connect to anything

  ◦   User(s) cannot connect to a specific server/application

- Determine whether this is a functionality or configuration problem

  ◦   User(s) can connect (gets a login screen or other response from the application server) but cannot log in (or get the expected response)

  ◦   User(s) can connect and log in but some or all functions are failing (for example, cannot send/receive e-mails)

- Determine whether this is a performance problem

  ◦   User(s) can connect, log in, and use the application normally; but it's slow

  ◦   The application works normally but sometimes it stalls and/or times out

Half-split troubleshooting and other logic

When I was doing component-level repair of electronic equipment early in my career, I learned to use the "half-split" troubleshooting method, which worked very well in almost every single case. Half-split troubleshooting is the process of cutting the problem domain (in my case, a piece of radio gear) in half by injecting or measuring signals roughly midway through the system. The idea is to see which half is working right and which half isn't, then shifting focus to the half that doesn't work, analyzing it halfway through, and so on. This process is repeated until you narrow the problem down to its source.

In the network and application world, the same half-split troubleshooting approach can be applied as well, in a general sense. If users are complaining that the network is slow, try to confirm or eliminate the network:

- Are users close to the server experiencing similar slowness? How about users in other remote locations?

- If a certain application is slow for a remote user, are other applications slow for that user as well?

- If users can't connect to a given server, can they connect to other servers nearby or at other locations?

By a process of logical examination of what does and doesn't work, you can eliminate a lot of guesswork and narrow your analysis down to just a few plausible possibilities.

It's usually much easier to determine the source of a connectivity or functionality problem if you have an environment where everything is working properly to compare with a situation that does not work. A packet capture of a working versus a non-working scenario can be compared to see what is different and if those differences are significant.

It is important not to make too many assumptions about a problem, even if the issue you're working on looks the same as the one that you've fixed before. Always verify the problem and the resolution that you should be able to apply and remove a fix and see the problem disappear/reappear reliably. Otherwise, you should question yourself about whether you've found the true source of the issue or are just affecting the symptoms.

Unless a reported problem is obviously a system-wide or specific server issue, it is better to conduct at least the initial analysis at or as close to the complaining user's workstation as possible. This has the advantages of offering the ability to perform the following actions:

- View and verify the actual problem that the user is reporting
- Measure round-trip times to the target server(s)
- Capture and view the TCP handshake process upon session initiation
- Capture and investigate the login and any other background processes and traffic
- Look for indications of network problems (lost packets and retransmissions) as they are experienced by the user's device
- Measure the apparent network throughput to the user's workstation during data downloads
- Eliminate the need to use a capture filter; the amount of traffic to/from a single workstation should not be excessive

A capture at a user workstation, server, or other device should be conducted with the use of an aggregating **Test Access Point** (**TAP**) versus using a switch SPAN port (as discussed in *Chapter 3, Capturing All the Right Packets*, or as a last resort by installing Wireshark on the user's workstation or server (if authorized).

Troubleshooting connectivity issues

Single user or small group connectivity issues can be resolved by confirming that the networking functions required for a user workstation to access local and remote network resources are functioning properly. The basic requirements or items to confirm include:

- Enabling the correct network interface(s) (workstation configuration)
- Confirming layer 1 (physical) connectivity
- Obtaining an IP address, subnet mask, and default gateway for each interface (DHCP)
- Obtaining the MAC address of the default gateway or other local network services (ARP)
- Obtaining the IP address of a network service (DNS)
- Connecting to a network service (TCP handshake or UDP response)

We'll briefly discuss each of these in order; while the first two steps will not involve using Wireshark, they are a necessary part in a troubleshooting approach. If the connectivity issue is affecting a group of users or a whole office, the first step is probably not applicable.

Enabling network interfaces

While it may seem obvious that network interfaces need to be enabled, the assumption that they are automatically enabled (especially for the wireless connectivity) by default upon device boot up may be false.

On Windows, you can use the command-line utility `ipconfig` to view the status and basic configuration (IP address, subnet mask, and default gateway) of network interfaces; on Linux or MAC devices, the equivalent command is `ifconfig` or `ip`.

Confirming physical connectivity

If a connectivity problem is isolated to a single user's workstation, the physical connections are suspected. There are a few items to check, and the troubleshooting steps that can be taken are as follows:

- If there is a problem with the Ethernet cable from the workstation to a wall jack, you need to swap the cable with a different one.
- If there is a problem with the cabling from the user's wall jack to the switch port, you need to temporarily plug the user's Ethernet cable into another (known good) wall jack.
- If there is a problem with the switch, switch port, or port configuration, you need to temporarily plug the user's port cable into another (known good) port. Be aware that some network security policies call to disable switch ports until they are needed or configuring the port to be associated with a single, specific MAC address. If so, a port may not work when you plug into it although there is nothing physically wrong with it.

Obtaining the workstation IP configuration

Unless the workstation was manually configured, it will need to get its IP address, subnet mask, default gateway, and DNS server settings from a DHCP server. If this does not appear to be working properly (after checking the configuration using `ipconfig` (Windows) or `ifconfig`, (Linux or Mac OS X)), you need to perform a packet capture during the workstation initialization/boot-up process using a TAP or SPAN port and investigate the DHCP requests and responses.

There are eight DHCP message types (not to be confused with the two Bootstrap Protocol types, Boot Request and Boot Reply):

Message type number	Message type	Description
1	DHCP Discover	A client broadcast to locate an available DHCP server
2	DHCP Reply	A server to client response to a DHCP Discover to offer configuration parameters
3	DHCP Request	A client message to a DHCP server to either one of the following conditions: • Request offered parameters from one server and decline offers from other DHCP servers • Confirm correctness of previously allocated address after a reboot • Extending the lease on an IP address
4	DHCP Decline	Client message to DHCP server indicating the offered address is not acceptable
5	DHCP Acknowledgment	Server to client with configuration parameters including a committed network address
6	DHCP Negative Acknowledgement	Server to client indicating client's address is incorrect or expired
7	DHCP Release	Client to server releasing a network address and canceling a lease
8	DHCP Informational	Client to server asking for local configuration parameters only

For a workstation that is booting up and was previously working on the network, you'll generally see the DHCP Request and Acknowledgment packets verifying that the workstation can still use a previously leased address. On an entirely cold start up, the first two DHCP packets will be DHCP Discover and DHCP Offer packets, followed by the Request and ACK packets.

In a DHCPv6 environment, the typical packet sequence is DHCPv6 Solicit, DHCPv6 Advertise, DHCPv6 Request, and DHCPv6 Reply.

The fields to verify in a DHCP Response packet (or similar fields in a DHCPv6 Advertise packet) include the following four fields:

- **Your (client) IP Address**: This is the offered IP address for this workstation
- **Subnet Mask**: This is the subnet mask to use on this network
- **Domain Name Server**: This is the DNS server IP address
- **Router**: This is the IP address of the default gateway to use

This is minimum data required for any network communications; an example of these fields being provided in a DHCP Reply packet is illustrated in the following screenshot:

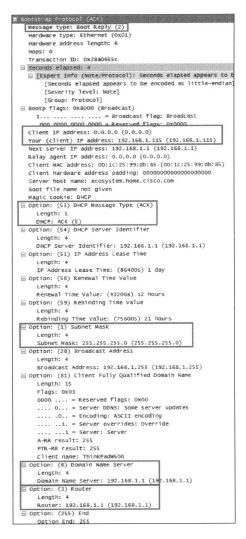

You can apply Wireshark display filters to isolate DHCP packets; the filter is
bootp, as this is the legacy name for DHCP:

- **DHCP display filter**: bootp   bootp.option.dhcp == 5
  (DHCP Message Type 'ACK')

- **DHCPv6 display filter**: dhcpv6   dhcpv6.msgtype == 2
  (DHCPv6 'Advertise')

You can save the basic bootp and dhcpv6 display filters as a **Filter Expression
Button (FEB)** after entering the filter string in the textbox on the **Display Filter**
toolbar, clicking on **Save**, and giving the button a name such as DHCP Pkts and
DHCPv6 Pkts respectively. Alternatively, you could combine both filters with an
or (||) in one button, as shown in the following screenshot:

You might want to save another FEB that displays an abnormal DHCP condition
packets using the following display filter string and call the **DHCP Errors** button
or a similar as follows:

```
bootp.option.dhcp == 4 || bootp.option.dhcp == 6 || bootp.option.dhcp
== 7
```

Similar abnormal event display filters for DHCPv6 could include:

```
dhcpv6.msgtype == 8 || dhcpv6.msgtype == 9 || dhcpv6.msgtype == 10
```

You can research more about DHCP, DHCPv6, and the various DHCPv6 message
types online or from other sources if you need to analyze these in more detail.

Obtaining MAC addresses

A workstation will utilize the ARP protocol to obtain a MAC address for known
IP addresses of network services, such as its default gateway or the DNS server if
it's located on the same network segment. The ARP protocol and how it typically
functions has already been covered in *Chapter 2, Networking for Packet Analysts*.

You may want to create an ARP FEB using the arp display filter syntax to make it
quick and easy to inspect those packets.

Obtaining network service IP addresses

A client workstation sends queries to a DNS server to obtain an IP address for a given hostname; the DNS server responds with the information or asks other DNS servers for the information on behalf of the client.

The format of the DNS query and response packet fields as displayed in the Wireshark **Packet Details** pane is fairly intuitive. An example of a DNS response packet containing a resolved IP address for time.windows.com, which actually provided the IP address (137.170.185.211) for the alias time.microsoft.akadns.com is shown in the following screenshot:

```
⊞ Frame 1116: 131 bytes on wire (1048 bits), 131 bytes captured (1048 bits) on int
⊞ Ethernet II, Src: c8:d7:19:21:b7:ec (c8:d7:19:21:b7:ec), Dst: 00:24:9b:06:8f:f9
⊞ Internet Protocol Version 4, Src: 192.168.1.1 (192.168.1.1), Dst: 192.168.1.125
⊞ User Datagram Protocol, Src Port: 53 (53), Dst Port: 59274 (59274)
⊟ Domain Name System (response)
     [Request In: 1115]
     [Time: 0.000580000 seconds]
     Transaction ID: 0xabf7
  ⊞ Flags: 0x8180 Standard query response, No error
     Questions: 1
     Answer RRs: 2
     Authority RRs: 0
     Additional RRs: 0
  ⊟ Queries
    ⊟ time.windows.com: type A, class IN
        Name: time.windows.com
        [Name Length: 16]
        [Label Count: 3]
        Type: A (Host Address) (1)
        Class: IN (0x0001)
  ⊟ Answers
    ⊟ time.windows.com: type CNAME, class IN, cname time.microsoft.akadns.net
        Name: time.windows.com
        Type: CNAME (Canonical NAME for an alias) (5)
        Class: IN (0x0001)
        Time to live: 774
        Data length: 27
        CNAME: time.microsoft.akadns.net
    ⊟ time.microsoft.akadns.net: type A, class IN, addr 137.170.185.211
        Name: time.microsoft.akadns.net
        Type: A (Host Address) (1)
        Class: IN (0x0001)
        Time to live: 78
        Data length: 4
        Address: 137.170.185.211 (137.170.185.211)
```

If a client workstation cannot obtain the IP address of a web service or application server, a packet-level investigation of the request (which URL or hostname is being requested), and what the response is from the DNS server (if any) should be revealing. A comparison of a failing query with queries that work properly for other hostnames or from other workstations should reveal the root of the problem (if DNS is the problem). Failure to obtain an IP address can be caused by an inoperable DNS server, improper hostname or URL, or a problem with connectivity from the user to other parts of the network, which we'll check next.

Basic network connectivity

A few simple tests can confirm that basic network connectivity is working, or reveal a routing issue or another issue that needs to be addressed by the network support team.

Capturing and analyzing the ICMP packets sent and received during the following tests can be revealing; although, the test results themselves are often telling enough:

- Ping the user's default gateway using the default gateway IP address obtained from using `ipconfig /all` (Windows) or `ip addr show` (Linux) to confirm that the user workstation has basic connectivity on the local network.

- Ping the hostname or URL of the target server. If this fails (request timed out message), try to ping other hosts or URLs. If necessary, inspect the DNS and/or ICMP responses in a packet capture of these tests to determine the nature of the failure. Otherwise, take note of the average round trip times.

- If a ping works to the default gateway but pinging other targets fails, a traceroute to a target server can reveal where in the network path connectivity ceases to function or is blocked.

 The traceroute command-line utility in Windows is `tracert`, whereas for traceroutes on Linux/Unix and Mac OS X machines, the command is `traceroute`. To do a traceroute in Windows, open a **Command Prompt (CMD)** window and type `tracert <hostname or IP Address of target>`. In most other environments, open a terminal window and type `traceroute <hostname or IP address of target>`.

If you can ping the target server and network connectivity is functioning, you can move on to the next step in the troubleshooting process. If not, be aware that some hosts may be configured to not respond to ICMP ping requests, and/or ICMP is blocked by a firewall between the user and server for security reasons. So, the inability to ping a device is not necessarily a sign of a network problem. Traceroute results should help determine how far and to what extent network connectivity is functioning in the path towards the target server; testing to other targets should be revealing as well.

An example of pinging a default gateway, then a URL, and finally performing a traceroute to the target URL is depicted in the following screenshot:

Connecting to the application services

If network connectivity from a user workstation to a target server is functional (as proven by the ability to ping the host), a problem connecting to a specific application hosted on that server may be caused by a number of factors:

- The URL or port used by the client to access the application is wrong
- The port used to access the application is blocked by a firewall
- The application service is not turned up or is not working properly

The first of these factors is far more likely for a single user issue. Any of the last two factors would prevent anyone in a group or the whole organization from accessing the application. A packet-level analysis (from the client side) of a user attempting to connect to an application that is blocked should result in ICMP messages: **Destination Host is Unreachable** or **Destination Port is Unreachable**, or there will be no response at all if ICMP messages are being blocked by a firewall.

If the server is up, the application is reportedly operational but cannot be accessed; a client-side capture does not offer any solid clues, but a packet capture of the TCP session setup (if any) from or near the server end should be revealing.

Troubleshooting functional issues

If a user is able to connect and set up a TCP session with an application server, but the application does not function otherwise, or function correctly, then, there are a number of areas that can be investigated. These areas can be investigated using a combination of packet-level analysis, error reports, and configuration comparisons with captures and configurations from other users' machines:

- **User credentials**: The most common reason for specific-user issues with application functionality is the lack of proper credentials, authorization, rights, and so on. This is the first thing to check whether other users are working normally.
- **Application settings on the user machine**: Some applications require specific configuration files to be placed on a user's machine in a specific location. Applications may also require certain version levels of application-specific utilities, Java, .NET frameworks, and so on. Usually, an application will provide an error message indicating at least the general nature of a configuration problem.
- **Application reported errors**: You can look for the error code within response packets or on the user screen that may reveal the nature of application errors:
  - Status code greater than 400 in HTTP, FTP, or SIP response packets
  - Error code in SMB response packets
  - Other application-specific exceptions, error codes, and messages

- **Differences in web browsers**: Some web applications are designed to work with specific browsers (Chrome, Internet Explorer, Firefox, Opera, and so on) and may not work properly or at all on other browsers and there may not be any error messages provided that indicate this is the case. A comparison of the browser type and version with other working users may be revealing.

The causes of network connectivity and application functionality issues can vary widely, so it is impossible to draw a clear roadmap for every possibility. The best approach to successfully address these problems is not to make too many assumptions without proving those assumptions correct with systematic, logical troubleshooting steps, but try to find or create a scenario where the system, or at least part of the system, works properly and compare the appropriate packet-level details of the working environment to the one that doesn't work.

Performance analysis methodology

Analyzing an application's performance problem is basically a case of identifying where the majority of the time for a particular task to complete is being spent, and measuring/comparing that time to what is normal and/or acceptable for that type of task.

Top five reasons for poor application performance

Generally speaking, performance issues can be attributed to one of the following five areas, in order of decreasing likelihood:

- Server processing time delay
- Application turns delay
- Network path latency
- Bandwidth congestion
- Data transport (TCP) issues

Client processing time is usually a relatively small component of overall response time—except perhaps for some compute-extensive desktop applications, which leaves the focus on the network and server environments and any performance-affecting application design characteristics.

Preparing the tools and approach

As was done when preparing to troubleshoot a connectivity or functionality problem, you'll need to gather the right information about the application environment and problem domain. You'll also want to determine which tools you may need to use during the analysis: Wireshark, TAPs to facilitate packet captures, and any other analysis tools.

You will also need to determine where to perform the first packet capture:

- A client-side capture is the best place to begin a performance analysis effort. From this vantage point, you can view and verify what the user is complaining about, view any error messages presented to the user or evident in the packet capture, measure network round-trip times, and capture the performance characteristics to study within a packet capture without the need to use a capture filter so you know you won't miss anything.
- A server-side capture may be needed because a client-side capture may not be possible for a user that is at a long distance, or to analyze server-to-server transactions to backend databases or other data sources.
- A packet capture at some intermediate point in the network path may be needed to isolate the source of excessive packet loss/errors and the associated retransmissions.

Remember that the use of an aggregating TAP is preferable over using SPAN ports, or you can install Wireshark on the client workstation or server as a last resort, but get the capture done any way you have to.

Performing, verifying, and saving a good packet capture

After performing the capture and saving the bulk capture file, confirm the following:

1. Check the file to ensure there are no packets with the **ACKed Unseen Segment** messages in the Wireshark **Warnings** tab in the **Expert Info** menu, which means Wireshark saw a packet that was acknowledged but didn't see the original packet; an indication that Wireshark is missing packets due to a bad TAP or SPAN port configuration or excessive traffic levels. In any case, if more than just a few of these show up, you'll want to do the capture again after confirming the capture setup.

2. Next, you'll want to review the captured conversations in **IPv4** in the **Conversations** window and sort the **Bytes** column. The IP conversation between the user and application server should be at or near the top so you can select this conversation, right-click on it, and select **A <-> B** in the **Selected** menu.

3. After reviewing the filtered data to ensure it contains what you expected, select **Export Specified Packets** from the **File** menu and save the filtered capture file with a filename that reflects the fact that this is a filtered subset of the bulk capture file.

4. Finally, open the filtered file you just saved so you're working with a smaller, faster file without any distracting packets from other conversations that have nothing to do with your analysis.

Initial error analysis

At the onset of your analysis, you should take a look through the **Errors, Warnings**, and **Notes** tabs of Wireshark's **Expert Info** window (**Analyze | Expert Info**) for significant errors such as excessive retransmissions, Zero Window conditions, or application errors. These are very helpful to provide clues to the source of reported poor performance.

Although a few lost packets and retransmissions are normal and of minimal consequence in most packet captures, an excessive number indicates that network congestion is occurring somewhere in the path between user and server, packets are being discarded, and that an appreciable amount of time may be lost recovering from these lost packets.

Seeing a high count number of Duplicate ACK packets in the **Expert Info Notes** window may be alarming, but can be misleading. In the following screenshot, there was up to 69 Duplicate ACKs for one lost packet, and for a second lost packet the count went up to 89 (not shown in the following screenshot):

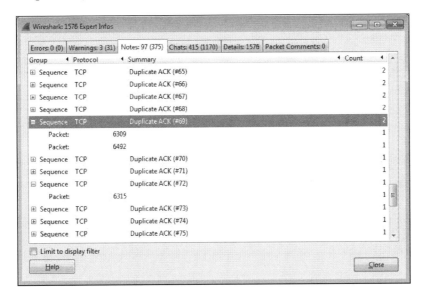

However, upon marking the time when the first Duplicate ACK occurred in Wireshark using the **Set/Unset Time Reference** feature in the **Edit** menu and then going to the last Duplicate ACK in this series by clicking the packet number in the **Expert Info** screen and inspecting a **Relative time** column in the **Packet List** pane, only 30 milliseconds had transpired. This is not a significant amount of time, especially if **Selective Acknowledgment** is enabled (as it was in this example) and other packets are being delivered and acknowledged in the meantime. Over longer latency network paths, the Duplicate ACK count can go much higher; it's only when the total number of lost packets and required retransmissions gets excessively high that the delay may become noticeable to a user.

Another condition to look for in the **Expert Info Notes** window includes the **TCP Zero Window** reports, which are caused by a receive buffer on the client or server being too full to accept any more data until the application has time to retrieve and process the data and make more room in the buffer. This isn't necessarily an error condition, but it can lead to substantial delays in transferring data, depending on how long it takes the buffer to get relieved.

You can measure this time by marking the TCP Zero Window packet with a time reference and looking at the elapsed relative time until a **TCP Window Update** packet is sent, which indicates the receiver is ready for more data. If this occurs frequently, or the delay between Zero Window and Window Update packets is long, you may need to inspect the host that is experiencing the full buffer condition to see whether there are any background processes that are adversely affecting the application that you're analyzing.

 If you haven't added them already, you need to add the **Relative time** and **Delta time** columns in the **Packet List** pane. Navigate to **Edit | Preferences | Columns** to add these. Adding time columns was also explained in *Chapter 4, Configuring Wireshark*.

You will probably see the connection reset (RST) messages in the **Warnings** tab. These are not indicators of an error condition if they occur at the end of a client-server exchange or session; they are normal indicators of sessions being terminated.

A very handy **Filter Expression** button you may want to add to Wireshark is a **TCP Issues** button using this display filter string as follows:

```
tcp.analysis.flags && !tcp.analysis.window_update && !tcp.analysis.
keep_alive && !tcp.analysis.keep_alive_ack
```

This will filter and display most of the packets for which you will see the messages in the **Expert Info** window and provide a quick overview of any significant issues.

Detecting and prioritizing delays

Since we're addressing application performance, the first step is to identify any delays in the packet flow so we can focus on the surrounding packets to identify the source and nature of the delay.

One of the quickest ways to identify delay events is to sort a **TCP Delta time** column (by clicking on the column header) so that the highest delay packets are arranged at the top of the packet list. You can then inspect the **Info** field of these packets to determine which, if any, reflect a valid performance affecting the event as most of them do not.

In the following screenshot, a **TCP Delta time** column is sorted in order of descending inter-packet times:

Frame #	Delta Time Disp ▼	WS Stream #	Info
4201	45.004102	2	[TCP Keep-Alive] 60351→8080 [ACK] Seq=27002 A
4309	44.990984	2	[TCP Keep-Alive] 60351→8080 [ACK] Seq=27002 A
			8080→60351 [RST, ACK] Seq=1 Ack=27003
3820	30.760486	2	GET /orion/js/breadcrumb.js.i18n.ashx?l=en-US
952	13.110531	2	GET /orion/js/jquery/jquery.cluetip.css.i18n.
2141	7.614162	2	GET /orion/images/Gradient-Green.gif HTTP/1.1
3738	5.811606	2	GET /ScriptResource.axd?d=MQTuTR1d4o6MBa82-pm
3202	3.812984	2	POST /Orion/NetPerfMon/MapService.asmx/GetMap
2211	2.843889	2	GET /orion/vim/styles/extjsfix.css.i18n.ashx?
3504	2.795273	2	GET /Orion/NetPerfMon/NodePopup.aspx?NetObjec
3691	1.908830	2	HTTP/1.1 200 OK (PNG)[Unreassembled Packet]
3519	1.048155	2	GET /Orion/NetPerfMon/NodeDetails.aspx?NetObj
3516	0.602610	2	GET /Orion/NetPerfMon/NodePopup.aspx?NetObjec

Let's have a detailed look at all the packets:

- The first two packets are the **TCP Keep-Alive** packets, which do just what they're called. They are a way for the client (or server) to make sure a connection is still alive (and not broken because the other end has gone away) after some time has elapsed with no activity. You can disregard these; they usually have nothing to do with the user experience.

- The third packet is a Reset packet, which is the last packet in the conversation stream and was sent to terminate the connection. Again, it has no impact on the user experience so you can ignore this.

- The next series of packets listed with a high inter-packet delay were **GETs** and a **POST**. These are the start of a new request and have occurred because the user clicked on a button or some other action on the application. However, the time that expired before these packets appear were consumed by the user think time—a period when the user was reading the last page and deciding what to do next. These also did not affect the user's response time experience and can be disregarded.

- Finally, **Frame # 3691**, which is a **HTTP/1.1 200 OK**, is a response from the server to a previous request; this is a legitimate response time of 1.9 seconds during which the user was waiting. If this response time had consumed more than a few seconds, the user may have grown frustrated with the wait and the type of request and reason for the excessive delay would warrant further analysis to determine why it took so long.

The point of this discussion is to illustrate that not all delays you may see in a packet trace affect the end user experience; you have to locate and focus on just those that do.

You may want to add some extra columns to Wireshark to speed up the analysis process; you can right-click on a column header and select **Hide Column** or **Displayed Columns** to show or hide specific columns:

- **TCP Delta (tcp.time_delta)**: This is the time from one packet in a TCP conversation to the next packet in the same conversation/stream

- **DNS Delta (dns.time)**: This is the time between DNS requests and responses

- **HTTP Delta (http.time)**: This is the time between the HTTP requests and responses

 You should ensure that **Calculate conversation timestamps** is enabled in the **TCP** option, which can be found by navigating to **Edit | References | Protocols**, so that the delta time columns will work properly.

While you're adding columns, the following can also be helpful during a performance analysis:

- **Stream # (tcp.stream)**: This is the TCP conversation stream number. You can right-click on a stream number in this column, and select **Selected** from the **Apply as a filter** menu to quickly build a display filter to inspect a single conversation.

- **Calc Win Size (tcp.window_size)**: This is the calculated TCP window size. This column can be used to quickly spot periods within a data delivery flow when the buffer size is decreasing to the point where a Zero Window condition occurred or almost occurred.

Server processing time events

One of the most common causes of poor response times are excessively long server processing time events, which can be caused by processing times on the application server itself and/or delays incurred from long response times from a high number of requests to backend databases or other data sources.

Confirming and measuring these response times is easy within Wireshark using the following approach:

1. Having used the sorted **Delta Time** column approach discussed in the previous section to identify a legitimate response time event, click on the suspect packet and then click on the **Delta Time** column header until it is no longer in the sort mode. This should result in the selected packet being highlighted in the middle of the **Packet List** pane and the displayed packets are back in their original order.

2. Inspect the previous several packets to find the request that resulted in the long response time. The pattern that you'll see time and again is:

    1. The user sends a request to the server.

    2. The server fairly quickly acknowledges the request (with a **[ACK]** packet).

    3. After some time, the server starts sending data packets to service the request; the first of these packets is the packet you saw and selected in the sorted **Delta Time** view.

The time that expires between the first user request packet and the third packet when the server actually starts sending data is the **First Byte** response time. This is the area where you'll see longer response times caused by server processing time. This effect can be seen between users and servers, as well as between application servers and database servers or other data sources.

In the following screenshot, you can see a **GET** request from the client followed by an ACK packet from the server 198 milliseconds later (**0.198651** seconds in the **Delta Time Displ** column); **1.9** seconds after that the server sends the first data packet (**HTTP/1.1 200 OK** in the **Info** field) followed by the start of a series of additional packets to deliver all of the requested data. In this illustration, a **Time Reference** has been set on the request packet. Looking at the **Rel Time** column, it can be seen that **2.107481** seconds transpired between the original request packet and the first byte packet:

Rel Time (formatted)	Delta Time Displ	WS Stream #	Source Address	Destination Addr	Info
REF	*REF*	2	192.168.1.115	10.1.1.125	GET /Orion/NetPerfMon/
0.198651	0.198651	2	10.1.1.125	192.168.1.115	8080→60351 [ACK] Seq=1
2.107481	1.908830	2	10.1.1.125	192.168.1.115	HTTP/1.1 200 OK (PNG)
2.107671	0.000190	2	10.1.1.125	192.168.1.115	8080→60351 [ACK] Seq=1

It should be noted that how the First Byte data packet is summarized in the **Info** field depends upon the state of the **Allow subdissector to reassemble TCP streams** setting in the **TCP** menu, which can be found by navigating to **Edit | Preferences | Protocols**, as follows:

- If this option is disabled, the First Byte packet will display a summary of the contents of the first data packet in the **Info** field, such as **HTTP/1.1 200 OK** shown in the preceding screenshot, followed by a series of data delivery packets. The end of this delivery process has no remarkable signature; the packet flow just stops until the next request is received.

- If the **Allow subdissector to reassemble TCP streams** option is enabled, the First Byte packet will be summarized as simply a **TCP segment of a reassembled PDU** or similar notation. The **HTTP/1.1 200 OK** summary will be displayed in the **Info** field of the last data packet in this delivery process, signifying that the requested data has been delivered. An example of having this option enabled is illustrated in the following screenshot. This is the same request/response stream as shown in the preceding screenshot. It can be seen in the **Rel Time** column that the total elapsed time from the original request to the last data delivery packet was **2.1097** seconds:

Rel Time (formatted)	Delta Time Displ	WS Stream #	Source Address	Destination Addr	Info
2.109764	0.000900	2	10.1.1.125	192.168.1.115	[TCP segment of a reass
2.109766	0.000002	2	10.1.1.125	192.168.1.115	HTTP/1.1 200 OK (PNG)

The **Reassemble SMB Transaction payload** setting in the SMB protocol preferences will affect how SMB and SMB2 responses are summarized in the **Info** field in like fashion to the related setting in the TCP protocol preferences.

In either case, the total response time as experienced by the user will be the time that transpires from the client request packet to the end of the data delivery packet plus the (usually) small amount of time required for the client application to process the received data and display the results on the user's screen.

In summary, measuring the time from the first request to the First Byte packets is the server response time. The time from the first request packet to the final data delivery packet is a good representation of the user response time experience.

Application turn's delay

The next, most likely source of poor response times—especially for remote users accessing applications over longer distances—is a relatively high number of what is known as application turns. An app turn is an instance where a client application makes a request and nothing else can or does happen until the response is received, after which another request/response cycle can occur, and so on.

Every client/server application is subject to the application turn effects and every request/response cycle incurs one. An application that imposes a high number of app turns to complete a task—due to poor application design, usually—can subject an end user to poor response times over higher latency network paths as the time spent waiting for these multiple requests and responses to traverse back and forth across the network adds up, which it can do quickly.

For example, if an application requires 100 application turns to complete a task and the **round trip time** (**RTT**) between the user and the application is 50 milliseconds (a typical cross-country value), the app turns delay will be 5 seconds:

```
100 App Turns X 50 ms RTT network latency = 5 seconds
```

This app turns' effect is additional wait (response) time on top of any server processing and network transport delays that is 5 seconds of totally wasted time. The resultant longer time inevitably gets blamed on the network; the network support teams assert that the network is working just fine and the application team points out that the application works fine until the network gets involved. And on it goes, so it is important to know about the app turns effects, what causes them, and how to measure and account for them.

Web applications can incur a relatively high app turn count due to the need to download one or more CSS files, JavaScript files, and multiple images to populate a page. Web designers can use techniques to reduce the app turn and download times, and modern browsers allow numerous connections to be used at the same time so that multiple requests can be serviced simultaneously, but the effects can still be significant over longer network paths. Many older, legacy applications and Microsoft's **Server Message Block (SMB)** protocols are also known to impose a high app turn count.

The presence and effects of application turns are not intuitively apparent in a packet capture unless you know they exist and how to identify and count them. You can do this in Wireshark for a client-side capture using a display filter:

```
ip.scr == 10.1.1.125 && tcp.analysis.ack_rtt > .008 && tcp.flags.ack
== 1
```

You will need to replace the `ip.src` IP address with that of your server, and adjust the `tcp.analysis.ack_rtt` value to the RTT of the network path between the user and server. Upon applying the filter, you will see a display of packets that represent an application turn, and you can see the total app turns count in the **Displayed** field in the center section of the Wireshark's **Status Bar** option at the bottom of the user interface.

If you measure the total time required to complete a task (first request packet to last data delivery packet) and divide that time into the time incurred for application turns (number of app turns X network RTT), you can derive an approximate app turn time percentage:

```
5 seconds app turns delay / 7.5 seconds total response time = 66% of RT
```

Any percentage over 25 percent warrants further investigation into what can be done to reduce either the RTT latency (server placement) or the number app turns (application design).

Network path latency

The next leading cause of high response times is network path latency, which compounds the effects of application turns as discussed in the preceding section, as well as affecting data transport throughput and how long it takes to recover from packet loss and the subsequent retransmissions.

You can measure the network path latency between a client and server using the ICMP ping packets, but you can also determine this delay from a packet capture by measuring the time that transpires from a client SYN packet to the server's SYN, ACK response during a TCP three-way handshake process, as illustrated in the following figure of a client-side capture:

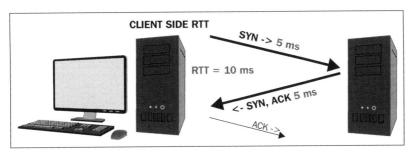

In a server-side capture, the time from the SYN, ACK to the client's ACK (third packet in the three-way handshake), also reflects the RTT. In practice, from any capture point, the time from the first SYN packet to the third ACK packet is a good representation of the RTT as well assuming the client and server response times during the handshake process are small. Be aware that the server response time to a SYN packet, while usually short, can be longer than normal during periods of high loading and can affect this measurement.

High network path latency isn't an error condition by itself, but can obviously have adverse effects on the application's operation over the network as previously discussed.

Bandwidth congestion

Bandwidth congestion affects the application's performance by extending the amount of time required to transmit a given amount of data over a network path; for users accessing an application server over a busy WAN link, these effects can become significant. A network support team should be able to generate bandwidth usage and availability reports for the in-path WAN links to check for this possibility, but you can also look for evidence of bandwidth congestion by using a properly configured Wireshark IO Graph to view network throughput during larger data transfers.

The following screenshot illustrates a data transfer that is affected by limited bandwidth; the flatlining at the 2.5 Mbps mark (the total bandwidth availability in this example), because no more bandwidth is available to support a faster transfer is clearly visible:

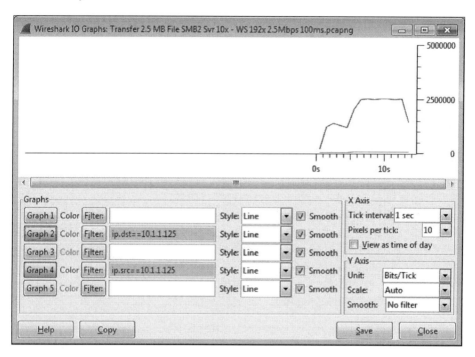

You can determine the peak data transfer rate in **bits-per-second (bps)** from an IO Graph by configuring the graph as follows:

- **X Axis Tick interval**: **1 sec**
- **Y Axis Unit**: **Bits/tick**
- **Graph 2 Filter**: `ip.dst == <IP address of server>`
- **Graph 4 Filter**: `ip.src == <IP address of server>`

These settings result in an accurate bits-per-second display of network throughput in client-to-server (red color) and server-to-client (blue color) directions. The **Pixels per tick** option in the **X Axis** panel, the **Scale** option in the **Y Axis** panel, and other settings can be modified as desired for the best display without affecting the accuracy of the measurement.

Be aware that most modern applications can generate short-term peak bandwidth demands (over an unrestricted link) of multiple Mbps. The WAN links along a network path should have enough spare capacity to accommodate these short term demands or response time will suffer accordingly. This is an important performance consideration.

Data transport

There are a number of TCP data transport effects that can affect application performance; these can be analyzed in Wireshark.

TCP StreamGraph

Wireshark provides TCP **StreamGraphs** to analyze several key data transport metrics, including:

- **Round-trip time**: This graphs the RTT from a data packet to the corresponding ACK packet.

- **Throughput**: These are plots throughput in bytes per second.

- **Time/sequence (Stephen's-style)**: This visualizes the TCP-based packet sequence numbers (and the number of bytes transferred) over time. An ideal graph flows from bottom-left to upper-right in a smooth fashion.

- **Time/sequence (tcptrace)**: This is similar to the Stephen's graph, but provides more information. The data packets are represented with an I-bar display, where the taller the I-bar, the more data is being sent. A gray bar is also displayed that represents the receive window size. When the gray bar moves closer to the I-bars, the receive window size decreases.

- **Window Scaling**: This plots the receive window size.

 The TCP StreamGraphs are unidirectional. You want to select a packet for the direction that is transporting data to get the proper view.

These analysis graphs can be utilized by selecting one of the packets in a TCP stream in the **Packet List** pane and selecting **TCP StreamGraph** from the **Statistics** menu and then one of the options such as the **Time-Sequence Graph (tcptrace)**.

The selected graph and **Control Window** will appear from the **Graph type** tab of the **Control Window** that you can select one of the other types of analysis graphs, as shown in the following screenshot:

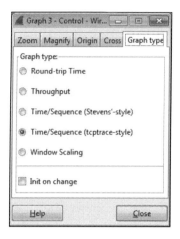

The **Time/Sequence Graph (tcptrace)** shown in the following screenshot plots sequence numbers as they increase during a data transfer, along with the gray receive window size line:

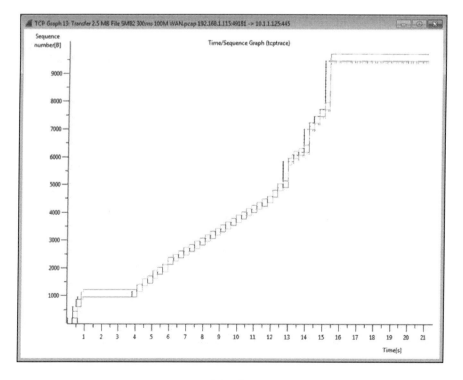

You can click and drag the mouse over a section of the graph to zoom into a particular section, or press the + key to zoom in and the - key to zoom out. Clicking on a point in any of the graphs will take you to the corresponding packet in the Wireshark's **Packet List** pane.

IO Graph

You can also analyze a the effects of TCP issues on network throughput by applying TCP analysis display filter strings to Wireshark's IO Graph, such as:

```
tcp.analysis.flags && !tcp.analysis.window_update
```

In the following screenshot of a slow SMB data transfer, it can be seen that the multiple TCP issues (in this case, packet loss, Duplicate ACKs, and retransmissions) in the red line correspond to a decrease in throughput (the black line):

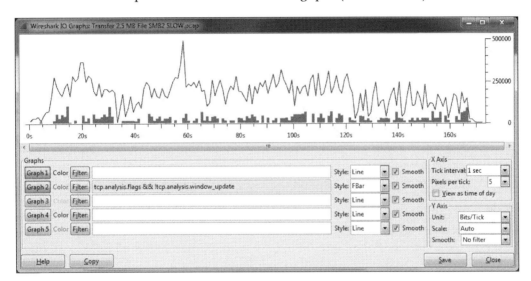

Clicking on a point in the IO Graph takes you to the corresponding packet in the Wireshark's **Packet List** pane so you can investigate the issue.

IO Graph – Wireshark 2.0

Wireshark 2.0, also known as Wireshark Qt, is a major change in Wireshark's version history due to a transition from the GTK+ user interface library to Qt to provide better ongoing UI coverage for the supported platforms. Most of the Wireshark features and user interface controls will remain basically the same, but there are changes to the IO Graph.

These are shown in the following screenshot, which shows the same TCP issues that were seen in the preceding screenshot:

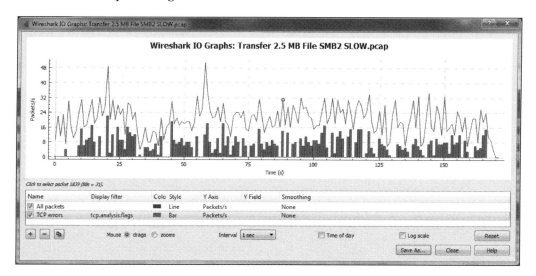

The new IO Graph window features the ability to add as many lines as desired (using the + key) and to zoom in on a graph line, as well as the ability to save the graph as an image or PDF document.

Summary

The topics covered in this chapter included troubleshooting methodology, how to use Wireshark to troubleshoot connectivity and functionality issues, performance analysis methodology, and the top five causes of poor application performance and how to use Wireshark to analyze those causes.

In the next chapter, we will review some of the common types and sources of malicious traffic and introduce how a security professional can use Wireshark to detect these threats.

7
Packet Analysis for Security Tasks

With the increasing threat of hackers, identity thieves, and corporate data theft, you need to be able to analyze the security of your network at the packet level.

The topics that will be covered in this chapter include:

- Security analysis methodology
- Scans and sweeps
- OS fingerprinting
- Malformed packets
- Phone home traffic
- Password cracking traffic
- Unusual traffic

Security analysis methodology

Security analysis at the packet level is based on detecting and analyzing suspect traffic, that is, the traffic that does not match normal patterns because of the presence of unusual protocol types or ports, or unusual requests, responses, or packet frequency. Suspicious traffic may include reconnaissance (discovery) sweeps, phone home behavior, denial of service attacks, botnet commands, or other types of behavior from direct attacks or virus- or botnet-based agents.

Wireshark captures strategic points in the network to investigate suspicious packets from specific hosts or on network segments and egress points can also complement any **Intrusion Detection System** (**IDS**) systems that may be in place to alert the IT staff about the suspicious traffic.

The importance of baselining

The ability to identify abnormal traffic patterns that bear investigation versus traffic caused by poorly behaving applications, misconfigurations, or faulty devices can be made much easier if you have a baseline of what is normal. A baseline is a snapshot capture of typical conversations with your primary applications and servers and the background traffic on the network segments that they reside on. In a potential security breach situation, you can compare the normal protocols, traffic patterns, and user sessions from a baseline with a current capture, filter out the normal traffic, and then inspect the differences.

To allow the comparison of baselines in your security analysis, you need to periodically capture and store packet trace files that cover a sufficient period of time to provide a good sample of typical user and background traffic patterns while keeping the file sizes manageable for use within Wireshark, for example, 100 MB to 1 GB per file. You can configure the **Ring Buffer** option within Wireshark's **Capture Options** window to save a series of reasonably sized files for longer captures or busier network segments.

Although your baselining needs and practices will depend on your environment, some of the traffic aspects that you should inspect include:

- Broadcast and multicast types and rates:
    - What devices and applications are using broadcasts and multicasts?
    - What are the typical broadcast and multicast packet rates?

- Applications and protocols:
    - What applications are running over the network?
    - What protocols and ports are they using?
    - Application launch sequences and typical tasks
    - Are application sessions encrypted?
    - Are all users forced to use encryption? Any exceptions?
    - What are the login/logout sequences and dependencies?

- Routing protocol(s) and routing updates
- ICMP traffic
- Boot-up sequences

- Name resolution sessions

- Wireless connectivity includes normal management, control, and data frame contents

- VoIP and video communications

- Idle time traffic is the host communicating with other hosts when there are no users logged in

- What backup processes are running at night and for how long?

- Are there any suspect protocols or broadcasts/scans taking place?

As you inspect your baseline captures, it is helpful to view a summary of the protocols being used by selecting **Protocol Hierarchy** from the Wireshark's **Statistics** menu. In the following screenshot, for example, you can see that there is some **Internet Relay Chat (IRC)** traffic, as well as the **Trivial File Transfer Protocol (TFTP)** traffic, neither of which might be normal on your network and could be an indication of rogue communications with outside entities:

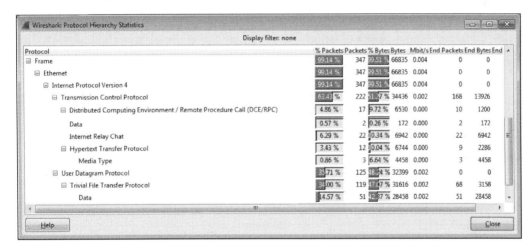

Analyzing baselines of normal traffic levels and patterns is also an excellent way of getting familiar with your network environment and its typical packet flows and protocols, which better prepares you to spot abnormal traffic.

Security assessment tools

There are several popular tools that are used by security professionals to perform security assessment and vulnerability testing. As these tools can generate the same types of scans, fingerprinting, and other exploitive activities, as might be used by hackers and malicious agents, they can be useful to a packet analyst to analyze the packets that they generate with Wireshark to build familiarity with how different types of activities appear in a packet trace and also to build display filters to detect them.

One of the most popular tools is **Network Mapper** (**Nmap**), a free and open source utility for network discovery and security auditing. Nmap runs on all major computer operating systems and offers a command-line and GUI version (**Zenmap**).

 You can find more information about Nmap at `http://nmap.org` and information on other top security tools can be found at `http://sectools.org`.

Identifying unacceptable or suspicious traffic

Wireshark can be used to identify unusual patterns or packet contents in the network traffic including network scans, malformed packets, and unusual protocols, applications, and or conversations that should not be running on your network. The following is a general list of traffic types that may not be acceptable and/or warrant investigation to validate their legitimacy in your environment:

- **MAC or IP address scans**: These attempt to identify active hosts on the network
- **TCP or UDP port scans**: These attempt to identify active applications and services

IP address and port scans can be generated from network management applications to build or maintain their list of devices and applications to monitor/manage, but that's usually the only legitimate source of these types of traffic.

- **Clear text passwords**: These are passwords that you can see in the Wireshark's **Packet Details** or **Packet Bytes** fields. These are typical for **File Transfer Protocol** (**FTP**) logins, but not typical or acceptable elsewhere.

- **Clear text data**: This is the data in packet payloads that can be read. This is typical for HTTP requests and responses and commonly seen in application server to database requests and responses, but these database exchanges should be between hosts on isolated, nonpublic network segments and otherwise physically secure environments.

- **Password cracking attempts**: These are repeated, systematic attempts to discover a working password, usually from a single device.

- **Maliciously formed packets**: These are packets with intentionally invalid or improperly formatted data in protocol fields that are intended to exploit vulnerabilities in applications.

- **Phone home traffic**: This is the traffic from a rogue agent that may be resident on a server or workstation that periodically checks in with a remote (usually off-network) host.

- **Flooding or Denial of Service (DOS) attacks**: This is the traffic that is intentionally sent at a very high packet-per-second rate to one or more hosts in an attempt to flood the host(s) or network with so much traffic that no one else can access their services.

- **Subversive activities**: These include a number of techniques to prepare for and facilitate the man-in-the-middle attacks where a device is tricked into sending packets to a malicious host for the purpose of intercepting data.

This is only a sampling of types of malicious traffic that you might see on your network; network security is an ever evolving exchange of increasingly sophisticated attacks and subsequent countermeasures.

As you develop your security analysis skills, you might want to build a special security profile in Wireshark that includes packet coloring rules based on display filters to help identify suspicious or malformed packets, as well as a set of **Filter Expression Buttons** that isolate and display various types of questionable traffic you might be looking for.

Some examples of display filters to isolate and inspect suspicious packets include:

Filter description	Display filter string
Detect ICMP pings and possible ping sweep	`icmp.type == 8 || icmp.type == 0`
ICMP destination unreachable filter (included redirects)	`(icmp.type >= 3 && icmp.type <= 5) || icmp.type == 11 || (icmpv6.type >= 1 && icmpv6.type <= 4)`
Unusual ICMP echo requests	`(icmp.type == 8) && !(icmp.code == 0x00)`

Filter description	Display filter string
TCP handshakes useful for detecting TCP scans as well as inspecting normal session setups/tear-downs/resets	`(tcp.flags&02 && tcp.seq==0) || (tcp.flags&12 && tcp.seq==0) || (tcp.flags.ack && tcp.seq==1 && !tcp.nxtseq > 0 && !tcp.ack >1) || tcp.flags.fin == 1 || tcp.flags.reset ==1`
Detect Xmas scan (URG, FIN, and PUSH flags set)	`tcp.flags == 0x029`
Other suspicious TCP settings: TCP SYN/ACK w/ Win size greater than 1025, SYN, FIN, PSH, URG bits set, no TCP flags set, TCP max segment size set to less than 1460	`((tcp.flags == 0x02) && (tcp.window_size < 1025)) || tcp.flags == 0x2b || tcp.flags == 0x00 || tcp.options.mss_val < 1460`
Internet Relay Chat (IRC) traffic (is this normal in your network?)	`tcp.port == 194 || (tcp.port >= 6660 && tcp.port <= 6669) || tcp.port == 7000`
High number of DNS answers (could be a list of command and control servers)	`dns.count.answers > 5`

Scans and sweeps

Malicious programs and rogue processes might investigate a network environment for available ports and hosts using various scanning processes before launching an exploit. Identifying the presence of these reconnaissance processes may allow thwarting the attack before it is launched, as well as tracking down and/or blocking the source of the malicious activity—especially if that source is inside the company as some of them are.

ARP scans

ARP scans, also called as ARP sweeps, are used to discover active localhosts on a network segment. An ARP sweep can be difficult to detect unless you apply a display filter and observe a steady, incremental sweep from the same device, as seen in the following screenshot:

No.	Time	Source	Destination	Protocol	Length	Info
20	3.550217	00:21:6a:86:0b:c2	Broadcast	ARP	42	who has 172.20.0.1? Tell 172.20.14.246
21	3.551628	00:21:6a:86:0b:c2	Broadcast	ARP	42	who has 172.20.0.4? Tell 172.20.14.246
22	3.551659	00:21:6a:86:0b:c2	Broadcast	ARP	42	who has 172.20.0.5? Tell 172.20.14.246
23	3.551687	00:21:6a:86:0b:c2	Broadcast	ARP	42	who has 172.20.0.6? Tell 172.20.14.246
24	3.551714	00:21:6a:86:0b:c2	Broadcast	ARP	42	who has 172.20.0.7? Tell 172.20.14.246
25	3.551742	00:21:6a:86:0b:c2	Broadcast	ARP	42	who has 172.20.0.8? Tell 172.20.14.246
26	3.551769	00:21:6a:86:0b:c2	Broadcast	ARP	42	who has 172.20.0.9? Tell 172.20.14.246
27	3.551797	00:21:6a:86:0b:c2	Broadcast	ARP	42	who has 172.20.0.10? Tell 172.20.14.246
28	3.551827	00:21:6a:86:0b:c2	Broadcast	ARP	42	who has 172.20.0.11? Tell 172.20.14.246
29	3.551855	00:21:6a:86:0b:c2	Broadcast	ARP	42	who has 172.20.0.12? Tell 172.20.14.246

As ARP packets cannot pass through a router, the source device conducting the ARP sweep must be on the same network segment that the ARP packets are seen on.

ICMP ping sweeps

ICMP ping sweeps are used to discover active hosts on local or remote network segments (since ICMP uses IP and is routable) using ICMP Type 8 Echo Requests and Type 0 Echo Replies for a range of IP addresses. You can easily detect ping sweeps by using a display filter `icmp.type == 8 || icmp.type == 0`.

TCP port scans

TCP port scans allow a malicious agent to discover which TCP ports are open on a target host. Network ports are the entry points to a server or workstation; a service that listens on a given port is able to service requests from a client. Malicious agents can sometimes exploit vulnerabilities in server code to gain access to sensitive data or execute malicious code on the machine, which is why testing all active ports is necessary for a complete coverage of any security validation.

Some of the most common ports used for TCP-based services include:

- 80 HTTP
- 443 HTTPS
- 8080 HTTP proxy
- 8000 HTTP alternate
- 21 FTP
- 22 SSH
- 23 Telnet
- 3389 Microsoft Remote Desktop
- 5900 VNC
- 25 SMTP
- 110 POP3
- 143 IMAP
- 3306 MySQL
- 1433 Microsoft SQL Server
- 1720 H.323
- 5060 SIP

A TCP port scan device will send a TCP SYN packet to a port on a target host, which will respond with either SYN, or ACK if the port is open, or RST if the port is closed. Similar to an ARP scan, a TCP scan can be detected by a series of SYN packets from a single IP address to a target IP address over a range of port numbers. A display filter can make detecting these types of scans easier:

```
ip.dest == <IP Address of target host> && tcp.flags.syn
```

UDP port scans

UDP port scans are like TCP scans, but they are run against typical UDP-based services, the most common of which include:

- 53 DNS
- 161/162 SNMP
- 67/68 DHCP
- 5060 SIP
- 135 Microsoft Endpoint Mapper
- 137/139 NetBIOS Name Service

The preceding topics cover just a sampling of the most common scans used by malicious agents. Security analysts should research this topic further to identify all the types of scans that may be used to exploit their particular environment's vulnerabilities.

OS fingerprinting

OS fingerprinting is a technique wherein a remote machine sends various types of commands to a target device and analyzes the responses to attempt to identify the target devices' operating system and version. Knowing which operating system a device is running makes it possible to use exploits specific to that operating system.

Nmap detects operating systems based on a series of port scans, ICMP pings, and numerous other tests, and then runs a set of follow-up tests based on the results to further define the OS version running.

In the following screenshot, you can see the test results verbiage from the GUI version of Nmap (Zenmap) as it completes an OS detection scan, as well as its best estimate of the operating system and version:

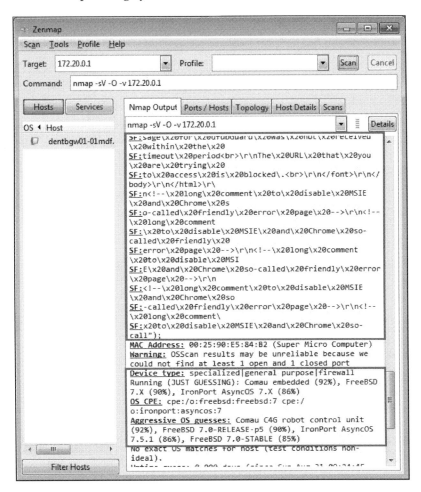

A Wireshark capture of the OS detection activity described earlier included as an example of one of the OS fingerprinting scripts that are run, a bogus HTTP request to the target device (172.20.0.1) for /nice%20ports%2C/Tri%6Eity.txt%2ebak to see exactly what kind of error response was generated, which is used to help pinpoint the OS version:

No.	Time	Source	Destination	Source Port	Destination Port	Protocol	Length	Info
2693	16.260887	172.20.14.246	172.20.0.1	2403	8080	HTTP	107	GET /nice%20ports%2C/Tri%6Eity.txt%2ebak HTTP/1.0
2694	16.262351	172.20.0.1	172.20.14.246	8080	2403	TCP	60	8080-2403 [ACK] Seq=1 Ack=54 Win=13080 Len=0
2695	16.262403	172.20.0.1	172.20.14.246	8080	2403	TCP	206	[TCP segment of a reassembled PDU]
2697	16.263793	172.20.0.1	172.20.14.246	8080	2403	HTTP	990	HTTP/1.0 200 OK (text/html)

The exact format of the HTML response from the preceding request could be used to identify the OS and/or web server version, as seen in the following Wireshark packet details screenshot:

```
Line-based text data: text/html
    <html>\r\n
    <head>\r\n
    <title>Error</title>\r\n
    </head>\r\n
    <body topmargin=1 leftmargin=1 marginheight=1 marginwidth=1 bgcolor="orange" text="black">\r\n
    <font size="+2">An error occurred. <br> </font>\r\n
    <font size="+1">\r\n
    This http server can only serve URL requests for ufdbGuard <br>\r\n
    redirection messages and does not understand the URL. <br>\r\n
    URL: <tt>/nice%20ports%2C/Tri%6Eity.txt%2ebak</tt> <br>\r\n
    Most likely the configuration of "redirect" statements is incorrect.  It should include "/cgi-bin/URLblocked.cgi". <br>\r\n
    </font>\r\n
    </body>\r\n
    </html>\r\n
    <!-- long comment to disable MSIE and Chrome so-called friendly error page -->\r\n
```

Analyzing packet captures of these kinds of OS fingerprinting requests and responses will make it much easier to spot similar activities from malicious entities.

Malformed packets

Maliciously malformed packets take advantage of vulnerabilities in operating systems and applications by intentionally altering the content of data fields in network protocols. These vulnerabilities may include causing a system crash (a form of denial of service) or forcing the system to execute the arbitrary code.

An example of malformed packet vulnerability is Cisco Security Advisory *cisco-sa-20140611-ipv6*, wherein vulnerability in parsing malformed IPv6 packets in a certain series of routers could cause a reload (reboot) of a certain card that carries network traffic, which could intermittently cause service outages.

Another example of this kind of vulnerability is in some unpatched Windows or Linux systems that will crash if they receive a series of fragmented packets where the fragments overlap each other.

The types and possibilities of malformed packets are endless, but vulnerabilities are usually announced as they are discovered and some may provide packet details. You can build display filters and/or build coloring rules in Wireshark to detect these packets. It also helps to study and understand what range of values the different protocol fields normally and legally contain, and what TCP and other protocol sequences normally look like so you can spot suspicious contents in packet flows.

Phone home traffic

Phone home traffic originates from a rogue application on a device that periodically connects to a remote (usually off-network) host to receive updates or commands or deliver data collected from the infected host. The majority of phone home traffic will be the operating system and virus protection updates, Dropbox or other external services, and similar authorized and appropriate services, so it will take some effort to identify malicious traffic out of this mix.

It is important to understand the risk that phone home traffic can represent: many botnet **Distributed Denial of Service (DDoS)** attacks are supported by a "zombie army" of hijacked computers running software that may lie undetected for some period of time except for periodic communications with their **Command and Control (C&C)** servers awaiting instructions to attack a target. In a similar fashion, keylogging traffic will send periodic reports of video screenshots and keystroke data to the collecting host.

One way to identify potentially malicious phone home traffic is to capture and inspect the DNS queries as these sessions start up, looking at two distinct areas:

- The hostname(s) of legitimate services are often reasonably recognizable.
- DNS queries for illegitimate applications contacting C&C servers will often return a long list of aliases with IP addresses that are not all in the same general range (that is, from all over the world). A display filter that helps identify DNS responses with long response lists is `dns.count.answers > 5`.

It also helps to have a baseline that includes the idle period traffic and a sample of known updates/services dialogs to compare a questionable capture to.

Password-cracking traffic

Password-cracking traffic can be detected by observing numerous error messages from a target host directed to a client that repeatedly and unsuccessfully attempts to log in. There are two general types of password cracking attempts:

- Dictionary attacks work from a list of common words, names, and numbers
- Brute force attacks use a sequence of characters, numbers, and key values

Both of these types are often thwarted by login security measures that lock out an account after a short number of failed login attempts.

Unusual traffic

While it is difficult to anticipate what methods a hacker may use in an attempt to infiltrate a network or host, there are a few things that should probably never happen on a normal, healthy network. Due to their usefulness in testing and conveying error conditions, ICMP packets are a likely target for malicious redirection. Since TCP is the predominant transport protocol in use for most applications, you should look out for abnormalities in TCP headers or payloads that could be a sign of malicious intent.

Some examples of abnormalities to look out for are discussed in the following table:

Suspicious content	Description
TCP bad flags	An illegal or unlikely combination of TCP flags. The SYN, SYN/ACK, ACK, PSH, FIN, and RST flags are normal when they're used in the appropriate places; anything otherwise warrants investigation.
SYN packet contains data	The initial TCP SYN packet should never contain payload data; it is used to establish a session only. Note, however, that the third ACK packet in the TCP can contain data.
Suspicious datagram payload contents	References to the operating system or other non-application directories, strange executables, or other payload data that doesn't seem to fit the purpose of the application being used to send the data.
Suspicious ping payload text	The text used to fill in the payload of an ICMP Echo Request packet is usually a benign sequential series of letters and numbers or similar meaningless text. If this text appears to carry commands or meaningful data, it warrants investigation.
Clear text passwords in FTP or Telnet sessions	Seeing FTP used to transport sensitive business data, or Telnet to administer switches and routers, isn't malicious intent by a hacker. It's negligent practice by employees as both protocols, by design, transmit clear text login IDs and passwords over the network, making it easy for even an unsophisticated hacker to capture them. There are **Secure FTP (sftp)** and **Secure Shell (SSH)** (Telnet alternative) solutions for all platforms available on the Web.

Summary

The topics covered in this chapter on security analysis included detecting scans and sweeps to identify targets for planned attacks, operating system fingerprinting, detecting malformed packets, and packets that are suspiciously fragmented or sent out of order, phone home traffic from malicious agents, identifying password cracking attempts, and identifying other abnormal packets and payloads.

In the next chapter, we'll review several key command-line utilities provided in a Wireshark installation, as well as a few additional packet analysis tools that can complement your toolset.

8
Command-line and Other Utilities

Wireshark includes a number of command-line utilities to manipulate packet trace files and offer GUI-free packet captures, and there are a few other tools that can help round out your analysis toolset.

The topics that will be covered in this chapter include:

- Capturing traffic with Dumpcap and Tshark
- Editing trace files with Editcap
- Merging trace files with Mergecap
- Other helpful tools

Wireshark command-line utilities

When you install Wireshark, a range of command-line tools also gets installed, including:

- `capinfos.exe`: This prints information about trace files
- `dumpcap.exe`: This captures packets and saves to a libpcap format file
- `editcap.exe`: This splits a trace file, alters timestamps, and removes duplicate packets
- `mergecap.exe`: This merges two or more packet files into one file
- `rawshark.exe`: This reads a stream of packets and prints field descriptions
- `text2pcap.exe`: This reads an ASCII hex dump and writes a libpcap file
- `tshark.exe`: This captures network packets or displays data from a saved trace file

The `Wireshark.exe` file launches the GUI version you're familiar with, but you can also launch Wireshark from the command line with a number of parameters; type `Wireshark -h` for a list of options and/or create shortcuts to launch Wireshark with any of those options.

 It is very helpful to add the Wireshark program directory to your system's PATH statement so that you can execute any of the command-line utilities from any working directory.

Capturing traffic with Dumpcap

The `dumpcap.exe` file is the executable that Wireshark actually runs under the covers to capture packets and save them to a trace file in libpcap format. You can run Dumpcap on the command line to circumvent using the Wireshark GUI and use fewer resources. A list of command-line options is available by typing `dumpcap.exe -h`.

Some of the most useful options are as follows:

- `-D`: This prints a list of available interfaces and exits
- `-i <interface>`: This specifies a name or index number of an interface to capture on
- `-f <capture filter>`: This applies a capture filter in the **Berkeley Packet Filter (BPF)** syntax
- `-b filesize`: This is the file size
- `-w <outfile>`: This is the name of the file where the files will be saved

An example of viewing a list of interfaces and then running Dumpcap to capture a specific interface with an IP address capture filter (note the use of quotes around the filter syntax) configured to use a three-file ring buffer with file sizes of 100 MB and an output filename derived from `capture.pcap` is illustrated in the following screenshot:

```
Command Prompt - dumpcap  -i 2 -f "host 192.168.1.115" -b filesize:100000 -b files:3 -w capture.pcap

C:\Wireshark>dumpcap -D
1. \Device\NPF_{ED5BF6FE-831D-4DED-A0BF-57E34BBDCBC0} (Wireless Network Connection 2)
2. \Device\NPF_{076F88E7-5E81-41A9-A610-4741FCA61E43} (Local Area Connection)
3. \Device\NPF_{865E114C-63A0-4853-A6CC-C6E1B4964655} (Wireless Network Connection)
4. \Device\NPF_{F6434602-A1E7-4BFD-AA1E-D2C2CA2CF1E0} (Bluetooth Network Connection)

C:\Wireshark>dumpcap -i 2 -f "host 192.168.1.115" -b filesize:100000 -b files:3 -w capture.pcap
Capturing on 'Local Area Connection'
File: capture_00001_20140904151641.pcap
Packets: 109012
```

You can get more information on Dumpcap options at `https://www.wireshark.`
`org/docs/man-pages/dumpcap.html`.

Capturing traffic with Tshark

Tshark can be used to capture network packets and/or display data from the capture
or a previously saved packet trace file; packets can be displayed on the screen or
saved to a new trace file.

The same syntax used to perform a basic capture using Dumpcap will work with
Tshark as well, so we won't repeat that here. However, Tshark offers a very wide
range of additional features, with a corresponding large number of command-line
options that can, as in all Wireshark utilities, be viewed by typing `tshark -h` in the
command prompt.

A number of Tshark options are to view statistics; an example of the command
syntax and statistical results from a capture (after pressing *Ctrl + C* to end the
capture) is illustrated in the following screenshot:

You will find an extensive number of details and examples on using statistics and other
Tshark options at `https://www.wireshark.org/docs/man-pages/tshark.html`.

Editing trace files with Editcap

You can use Editcap to split a trace file that is too large to work with in Wireshark into multiple smaller files, extract a subset of a trace file based on a start and stop time, alter timestamps, remove duplicate packets, and a number of other useful functions.

Type `editcap -h` in the command prompt for a list of options. The syntax to extract a single packet or a range of packets by packet numbers is as follows:

```
editcap  -r  <infile>  <outfile>  <packet#> [- <packet#>]
```

You must specify `<infile>` and `<outfile>`. The `-r` specifies to keep, not delete, the specified packet or packet range, for example:

```
editcap  -r  MergedTraces.pcapng   packetrange.pcapng   1-5000
```

You can split a source trace file into multiple sequential files, each containing the number of packets specified by the `-c` option:

```
editcap  -c 5000  MergedTraces.pcapng   SplitTrace.pcapng
```

You can eliminate duplicate packets in a file within a five-packet proximity:

```
editcap  -d  hasdupes.pcapng  nodupes.pcapng
```

If you have two trace files that have a significant span of time between them, and you want to merge them into one file but closer together, you can investigate all of the packets within one IO Graph or a similar analysis function; you can first use the `-t` option on one of the files to adjust the timestamps in that file by a constant amount (in seconds). For example, to subtract 5 hours from a trace file's timestamps, use the following command:

```
editcap  -t  -18000  packetrange.pcapng   adj_packetrange.pcapng
```

Comparing the two traces in Wireshark reveals the following details:

- **Packet #500 before adjustment**: `2014-09-04 15:27:38.696897`
- **Packet #500 after adjustment**: `2014-09-04 10:27:38.696897`

You can get more information on and examples of Editcap options at `https://www.wireshark.org/docs/man-pages/editcap.html`.

Merging trace files with Mergecap

You can use Mergecap to merge two or more trace files into one file. The basic syntax is as follows:

```
mergecap -w <outfile.pcapng>  infile1.pcapng   infile2.pcapng  …
```

For example:

```
mergecap -w merged.pacap   source1.pcapng   source2.pcapng    source3.
pcapng
```

One useful option you sometimes may want to use in Mergecap (and several of the other command-line utilities) is `-s <snaplen>`. This will truncate the packets at the specified length past the start of each frame, resulting in a smaller file; a typical value for `<snaplen>` is 128 bytes:

```
mergecap -w merged_trimmed.pcapng  -s 128  source1.pcapng  source2.pcapng
```

Mergecap batch file

If the capture files you want to merge have a variety of naming formats, you can create a `MergeTraces.bat` file containing the following Windows batch commands:

```
@echo off
cls
echo MergeTraces.bat
echo.
echo Merges multiple packet trace files with a .pcapng extension into one
.pcapng file
echo.
echo Usage: Copy MergeTraces.bat into the directory with the .pkt files
and execute
echo The utility will generate a 'MergedTraces.pcap' file
echo and a 'MergedFileList.txt' file which lists the .pcapng files
processed.
echo.
echo.
echo IMPORTANT!! You must type 'CMD /V:ON' from this window which enables
echo 'Delayed environment variable expansion' in order to properly
execute
echo this batch utility.
echo.
```

```
echo You must also add the path to Wireshark's mergecap.exe to your path
statement.
echo.
echo If you've not done this, Type Ctrl-C to exit; Otherwise
pause
echo.
echo Deleting old MergedFileList.txt...
if exist "MergedFileList.txt" del MergedFileList.txt
for %%f in (*.pcap-ng) do echo "%%f" >> MergedFileList.txt
echo Deleting old MergedTraces.pcapng...
if exist "MergedTraces.pcapng" del MergedTraces.pcapng
echo Preparing to merge:
echo.
type MergedFileList.txt
echo.
echo Merging.........
set FILELIST=
for %%f in (*.pcap-ng) do set FILELIST=!FILELIST! %%f
:: DEBUG
:: echo %FILELIST%
mergecap -w MergedTraces.pcapng %FILELIST%
echo.
if exist MergedTraces.pcapng @echo Done!
if NOT exist MergedTraces.pcapng @echo Error!! -- Check your settings.
echo.
```

Copy the batch file into a directory containing just the packet trace files you want to merge and execute it. The batch file will merge all the .pcapng files into one file called MergedTraces.pcapng. This is much easier than trying to specify a long list of unique source files in a command line, especially if the filenames contain date-time stamps. If you need to work with the .pcap files, change all instances of .pcapng to .pcap in the batch commands; you can also alter the output filename as desired.

You can also merge trace files by clicking-and-dragging the files into the Wireshark desktop. The files will be merged in chronological order based on their timestamps after selecting **Merge** from the Wireshark **File** menu. This works reasonably well as long as the total file size doesn't exceed 1GB.

You can get more info and examples of Mergecap options at https://www.wireshark.org/docs/man-pages/mergecap.html.

Other helpful tools

Wireshark is an extremely versatile and useful tool. However, there are some things it doesn't do easily or at all, so we'll discuss a few other tools you may want to include in your analysis toolset.

HttpWatch

HttpWatch is a packet-based performance analysis utility that integrates with Internet Explorer and Firefox browsers to view a graphical depiction and statistical values from HTTP interactions between the browser and websites. This kind of utility makes it easy to discover and measure from the user's perspective when significant delays are occurring and the source of those delays.

The following screenshot shows the HttpWatch visual and numerical analysis by loading the `www.wireshark.org` home page:

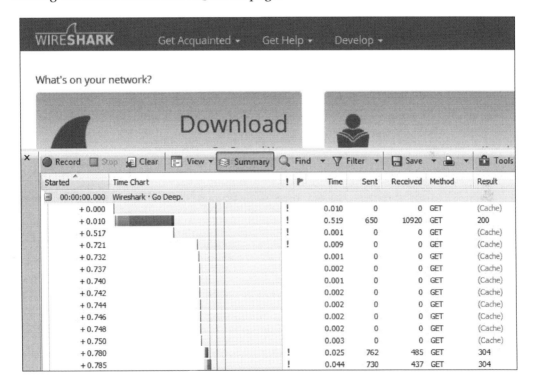

You can get more information about HttpWatch from `http://www.httpwatch.com/`. Also, a similar performance analysis utility is Fiddler, which can be found at `http://www.telerik.com/fiddler`.

SteelCentral Packet Analyzer Personal Edition

SteelCentral Packet Analyzer (previously known as Cascade Pilot) is available in Standard and Personal Edition versions. Unlike Wireshark, this utility is able to open and analyze multigigabyte trace files; you can quickly isolate a conversation of interest, right-click on it, and save that conversation in a separate packet trace file or launch Wireshark directly and pass that conversation to it from the same menu.

In addition, the utility offers a variety of network analysis screens called **Views** that provide graphical displays and reports on a wide range of performance perspectives. The following screenshot illustrates a set of **MAC Overview** Views:

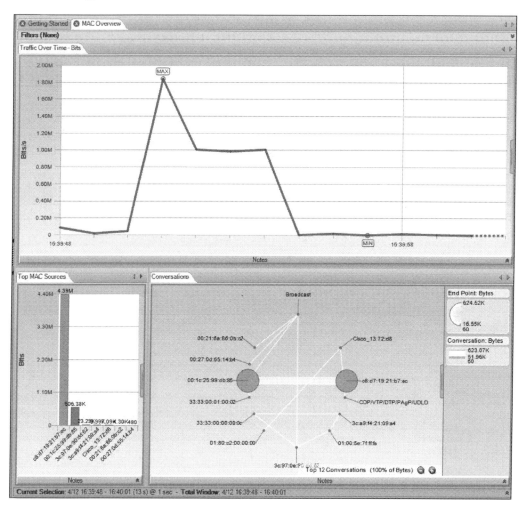

You can get more information on the SteelCentral Packet Analyzer products at `http://www.riverbed.com/products/performance-management-control/network-performance-management/packet-analysis.html`.

AirPcap adapters

If you are using Wireshark to analyze wireless networks, you will need a wireless adapter that provides the ability to see all of the available channels and provides a Radiotap Header, which offers additional information for each frame such as radio channel and signal/noise strengths.

The prevalent wireless adaptor for use with Wireshark or SteelCentral Packet Analyzer on Windows platforms is the **Riverbed AirPcap adapter**, which is available from the Riverbed website. The AirPcap adapter plugs into a USB port and includes drivers to integrate with Wireshark and provide the Radiotap Header information. There are several product models that offer increasing coverage of the various WLAN bands; AirPcap Nx offers the widest coverage. The following image depicts two of the available adapters:

You can get more information on the Riverbed AirPcap adapters at `http://www.riverbed.com/products/performance-management-control/network-performance-management/wireless-packet-capture.html`.

Summary

The topics covered in this chapter included several of Wireshark's command-line utilities to capture packets and edit and merge packet trace files, as well as several useful tools to compliment your analysis toolset.

This is the final chapter of this book on Wireshark. I hope you enjoyed reading it, and mostly, I hope you use it as a foundation to become a Wireshark expert!

Index

Z

Thank you for buying
Wireshark Essentials

About Packt Publishing

Packt, pronounced 'packed', published its first book *"Mastering phpMyAdmin for Effective MySQL Management"* in April 2004 and subsequently continued to specialize in publishing highly focused books on specific technologies and solutions.

Our books and publications share the experiences of your fellow IT professionals in adapting and customizing today's systems, applications, and frameworks. Our solution based books give you the knowledge and power to customize the software and technologies you're using to get the job done. Packt books are more specific and less general than the IT books you have seen in the past. Our unique business model allows us to bring you more focused information, giving you more of what you need to know, and less of what you don't.

Packt is a modern, yet unique publishing company, which focuses on producing quality, cutting-edge books for communities of developers, administrators, and newbies alike. For more information, please visit our website: www.packtpub.com.

About Packt Open Source

In 2010, Packt launched two new brands, Packt Open Source and Packt Enterprise, in order to continue its focus on specialization. This book is part of the Packt Open Source brand, home to books published on software built around Open Source licenses, and offering information to anybody from advanced developers to budding web designers. The Open Source brand also runs Packt's Open Source Royalty Scheme, by which Packt gives a royalty to each Open Source project about whose software a book is sold.

Writing for Packt

We welcome all inquiries from people who are interested in authoring. Book proposals should be sent to author@packtpub.com. If your book idea is still at an early stage and you would like to discuss it first before writing a formal book proposal, contact us; one of our commissioning editors will get in touch with you.

We're not just looking for published authors; if you have strong technical skills but no writing experience, our experienced editors can help you develop a writing career, or simply get some additional reward for your expertise.

Network Analysis Using Wireshark Cookbook

ISBN: 978-1-84951-764-5   Paperback: 452 pages

Over 80 recipes to analyze and troubleshoot network problems using Wireshark

1. Place Wireshark in the network and configure it for effective network analysis.

2. Use Wireshark's powerful statistical tools and expert system for pinpointing network problems.

3. Use Wireshark for troubleshooting network performance, applications, and security problems in the network.

Learning Kendo UI Web Development

ISBN: 978-1-84969-434-6   Paperback: 288 pages

An easy-to-follow practical tutorial to add exciting features to your web pages without being a JavaScript expert

1. Learn from clear and specific examples on how to utilize the full range of the Kendo UI toolset for the Web.

2. Add powerful tools to your website supported by a familiar and trusted name in innovative technology.

3. Learn how to add amazing features with clear examples and make your website more interactive without being a JavaScript expert.

Please check **www.PacktPub.com** for information on our titles

Instant Wireshark Starter

ISBN: 978-1-84969-564-0   Paperback: 68 pages

A quick and easy guide to getting started with network analysis using Wireshark

1. Learn something new in an Instant!
    A short, fast, focused guide delivering immediate results.

2. Documents key features and tasks that can be performed using Wireshark.

3. Covers details of filters, statistical analysis, and other important tasks.

Instant Traffic Analysis with Tshark How-to

ISBN: 978-1-78216-538-5   Paperback: 68 pages

Master the terminal-based version of Wireshark for dealing with network security incidents

1. Learn something new in an Instant!
    A short, fast, focused guide delivering immediate results.

2. Terminal-based version of Wireshark for dealing with network security incidents.

3. Useful filters to quickly identify and limit network problems derived from malware and a variety of network attacks.

Please check **www.PacktPub.com** for information on our titles

Made in the USA
Middletown, DE
25 August 2020